Everyday EVANGELISM *for* CATHOLICS

Everyday EVANGELISM CATHOLICS

Cathy Duffy

TAN Books
Charlotte, North Carolina

Cover design by Caroline K. Green

Cover image: Blurred background of talking people in restaurant © ChartsTable789 / Shutterstock

Library of Congress Control Number: 2018950328

ISBN: 978-1-5051-1235-1

Published in the United States by
TAN Books
PO Box 410487
Charlotte, NC 28241
www.TANBooks.com

Printed in the United States of America

CONTENTS

INTRODUCTION

Evangelism is a hot topic in the Catholic world today thanks to Pope Francis and his predecessors. But for at least a few centuries, most Catholics thought that evangelism was something Protestants do, not Catholics! Since the idea is so foreign to most Catholics, they have no idea where to start. I find that many Catholics would like to be involved in evangelism, but they need concrete ways of going about it.

I wrote *Everyday Evangelism for Catholics* to discuss how we can practice personal evangelism on a practical, everyday level—the sort of evangelism that most of us should be doing. Everyday evangelism includes the conversation with your relative who has left the Church, your friend who just doesn't get why you bother going to Mass every Sunday, your acquaintance who is grieving over the death of his mother, or your coworker who is making all of the wrong life choices and can't figure out why she's not happy. Conversations that arise from everyday issues often open doors for evangelism. But that does not mean you grasp *every* opportunity to tell people they need to start going to church. True evangelism is usually more subtle and time consuming, as you will soon see.

My Background

My enthusiasm for evangelism has a long history. I was a cradle Catholic who, like so many others, left the Church as a young adult. After a few years of trying to ignore God, I ended up reconnecting with the Catholic Church briefly. However, while my relationship with God was on much stronger ground at that point, my theological formation was not.

I readily joined my husband when he decided that Calvary Chapel sounded appealing. I developed an evangelistic outlook during the twenty plus years I detoured from Catholicism into the Protestant world. Protestants talk a great deal about evangelism and many of them expect all Christians to be evangelists. As I became more and more attuned to evangelism, I found opportunities galore to practice it. At first, my conversations occurred more frequently with those close to Christianity in some way. As you can read in chapter 8, my circles gradually broadened, and within those wider circles came many evangelizing opportunities.

When I returned to the Catholic Church, I brought with me my evangelistic outlook. I soon began volunteering to work with the RCIA (Rite of Christian Initiation for Adults) process in our parish. Within a few years, I was on staff running RCIA. One of the things I love most about the RCIA process is working with individuals. I enjoy hearing their stories, discussing their burning questions, and helping them fall in love with Jesus and his Church. (Along the way, I also picked up responsibility for adult faith formation, an opportunity to practice the new evangelization parish wide.)

Outside the Church, I found myself frequently involved in conversations about deep spiritual issues with people, both those I knew well and those I'd just met. Some of my most memorable conversations about spiritual issues have been with seatmates on long airplane flights! Working within the RCIA process helped me learn how to listen and ask good questions—both of which are key for having a worthwhile conversation.

As much as I enjoyed directing RCIA, I reached a point with my job where I was spending far more time on administration than in one-on-one conversations. I ended up resigning, but I continue to serve as a volunteer in my parish doing things that better fit my talents and bring me great delight.

One of these things is serving on our evangelism team, helping to plan parish efforts centered particularly on the Alpha program and our follow-up Discipleship Groups. (Alpha is an introductory evangelism course that is non-denominational but approved by the Catholic Church. See alphausa.org/catholic/ for more information.) In addition, I host a "Got Faith Questions" table in the church courtyard most Sunday mornings through the four morning Masses. Think of Lucy's "psychiatry" booth from the *Peanuts* cartoon strip. The table functions in a number of ways. I have a small sign that reads "Free books" and a few books from the Dynamic Catholic ministry sitting out. I keep a selection suitable for different needs—books such as *Rediscovering Catholicism, Rediscover Jesus, The Real Story* (short version of salvation history in Scripture), and *Catholic and Christian*, plus the *Pillar of Fire, Pillar of Truth* pamphlets.

Some people approach the table looking for a free book.

It's an excuse for me to say something like, "We've got books for people who are at different places on their faith journey. Let's see what would be most helpful to you." That allows at least a brief discussion about which book or pamphlet might be helpful. Sometimes it turns into a lengthy conversation about their spiritual journey. People approach the table with all sorts of questions from "Where's the restroom?" to "I haven't been to church in thirty years. What do I need to do?"

We occasionally have non-Catholic visitors as well. Some of them have been interested enough to engage in deep conversation about Catholicism, and at least a few are on their way into the Church. I've even been able to pray with some right there at the table. The "Got Faith Questions" table has turned out to be a fabulous evangelism tool.

I share all of this so that you can understand the diversity of experience I have had with evangelism. Our parish is on a "Divine Renovation" track. (Fr. James Mallon's book *Divine Renovation* has influenced many Catholic parishes which have prioritized mission over maintenance.) We are working to become a parish of intentional Catholics who understand that our primary mission is making disciples. It seems clear that at our parish there is definitely more interest in evangelism than ever before.

However, strategies for evangelism are unfamiliar to most Catholics. Many Catholics worry that they need to be firmly grounded in apologetics before they can evangelize. They fear they don't know enough and don't want to be pushy. They have no idea how to even begin the conversation. My hope is that this book will bridge the gap so that they will learn how to have evangelistic conversations in everyday situations and that it will become easy and comfortable for them to do so.

Givens That I'm Assuming

Many other books have been written about other aspects of evangelism, so I'm going to skim over some basic principles of evangelism that I expect most of my readers will have already encountered.

- We can't share a faith that we don't have ourselves. Only if we have a real relationship with Jesus can we share it with others.

- Evangelism needs to be motivated by love for others. We need to care enough for others that we want them to have a relationship with Jesus.

- Prayer is an essential component of evangelism. Ultimately, people are changed spiritually by the work of the Holy Spirit, not by our own wisdom, intelligence, winsomeness, or any other talents we possess. We must pray continually for broad efforts in evangelism as well as for those people we personally hope to bring into relationship with Christ. Without prayer, we labor in vain. To that end, please consider using the focusing prayers at the beginning of each chapter.

- We need to walk our talk. Nothing undermines our evangelistic efforts as much as actions that contradict the message of the Gospel.

- Evangelism is a calling for all God's people. It might be through cloistered prayer, service, or active engagement, but all Christians are called to share the good news of salvation through Jesus Christ.

If you want more information on these aspects of evangelism, I recommend the following books:

- *Forming Intentional Disciples* by Sherry A. Weddell, Our Sunday Visitor.

- *The Joy of the Gospel* (Pope Francis's encyclical *Evangelii Guadium*), available on the Vatican's website.

- *Nudging Conversions: A Practical Guide to Bringing Those You Love Back to the Church* by Carrie Gress, Beacon Publishing.

As you dive further into this book, you'll see plenty of other suggested reading and videos to watch concerning various aspects of evangelization. A complete list of these books can be found in the "Recommended Reading and Resources" section.

CHAPTER 1

THE CENTRALITY
OF EVANGELISM

God our Father and fount of all love, please develop in
us a love for others that gives us the desire and courage
to share the good news of salvation. We ask this in the
name of Jesus Christ, your precious son. Amen.

Some Catholics are beginning to say that evangelism is their top priority. Some credit this burst of evangelistic enthusiasm to Pope Francis's call for the Church to become more mission-minded by sharing the Gospel with others as presented in his encyclical *Evangelii Gaudium* (*The Joy of the Gospel*). In July 2017, at the Convocation of Catholic Leaders in Orlando, Florida, *National Catholic Register* reporter Matthew Bunson observed, "In virtually every speech they heard the importance of missionary discipleship and the urgency of the task of evangelization."[A]

While evangelism has been part of the Catholic faith since Jesus gave the Great Commission in Matthew 28, emphasis has waxed and waned. We have seen periods when the

7

Church seemed comfortably ensconced in maintenance mode and other times, such as in the post-Reformation period, when explosive evangelistic efforts brought many back to Catholicism.

For Catholicism in the United States in the twentieth century, maintenance mode seemed the norm. We left evangelism to the Protestants, the Mormons, and the Jehovah Witnesses. Immigration and the baby boom brought plenty of people to the pews without any evangelistic efforts. Consequently, it seems that the general attitude was, "Why bother?"

Many had forgotten that evangelism—sharing the good news of the Gospel with others—is the mission of the Church. Too many Catholics assumed that catechizing those who were already there was the extent of their evangelistic responsibility. They catechized through schools and from the pulpit, but serious catechesis was reserved for those preparing for the sacraments of initiation, especially for First Communion and Confirmation. Many families abandoned personal responsibility for catechizing their own children, instead expecting the Church to provide that service. With the focus primarily on sacramental catechesis, many Catholics failed to realize that those attending church were rarely, if ever, asked if they believed in God, much less whether they believed in the Incarnation, salvation through Jesus's death on the cross, the Resurrection, and other essentials. Those beliefs were just assumed to be present. Even though parishioners would repeat baptismal vows on occasion or recite the Nicene or Apostles' Creed, some did so only because that was what everyone else was doing rather than as a statement of their own faith.

Saying It Is One Thing. Doing It Is Another.

The New Evangelization—the call for new methods of evangelization as well as to re-evangelize those who are still technically considered Catholic but whose lives provide no evidence to back it up—is a response to that reality. The Church finally realized that the presentation of the *Kerygma*—the basic message of the Gospel—needed to be revitalized for modern audiences. The Church also recognized that being baptized Catholic, calling oneself a Catholic, or even coming to Mass every weekend does not guarantee that a person has a relationship with Jesus Christ. Add these souls to the millions of baptized Catholics who have walked away and do not even pretend to be Catholic any longer, and it paints a grim picture. Some have left to join other non-Catholic churches, but Protestants these days are experiencing the same membership-bleed as Catholics, so there are deeper cultural forces at work. Many baptized Catholics (as well as former Protestants) now consider themselves atheists, "spiritual-but-not-religious," or the increasingly popular "none."

We use the term *lapsed* to describe Catholics who have walked away from the Faith, but that seems a bit inadequate. *Lapsed* implies that maybe this is a membership that could easily be reinstated tomorrow, just as a lapsed subscription can be. However, the gulf separating many lapsed Catholics from their faith is often gigantic, a Grand Canyon rather than a gully.

While the new evangelization in the United States has focused heavily upon baptized Catholics who are not practicing their faith, it is only a starting point. We need to be concerned about everyone. After all, the Great Commission of Matthew 28 says that we are to "make disciples of all nations." This clearly implies that the mission field includes all of the people in all of the nations. If Catholics truly believe the good news of the Gospel—that God loves each one of us so much that he sent his son to die for our sins so that we can have eternal life—then out of love for others, we should be anxious to share the Good News with them.

The Great Commission

"Go, therefore, and make disciples of all nations, baptizing them in the name of the Father, and of the Son, and of the holy Spirit, teaching them to observe all that I have commanded you." Matthew 28:19–20a

However, it's seems fairly obvious that there is not much point in trying to evangelize the unbaptized and unchurched, only to bring them into a church where too many attendees seem to be there under duress. How inspiring and uplifting is it to be seated next to someone at Mass who is not participating, who continually checks her cell phone, and who arrives late and leaves early? Given this unfortunate reality, we need to first re-evangelize those in the pews or those who visit those pews only on Christmas and Easter or for funerals and weddings.

From the parish level, this is critical to understand. Evangelism generally needs to happen from the inside out. You cannot replenish your dying parish to any significant degree by attempting to pull in new members from among the unbaptized or other Christian denominations. They won't find it any more attractive to be there than will your reluctantly-attending parishioners. New Christians want and need to be around other Christians who are what Matthew Kelly describes as "dynamic Catholics." These are Catholics who visibly exhibit the characteristics of prayer, study, generosity, and evangelism. They have a heart for others that enables them to be warm and welcoming to newcomers. They help create an environment that is attractive to those investigating Christianity and Catholicism in particular.

"Missionary disciples" is another term that is increasingly being used to describe those who have responded to the call of the Gospel themselves and who have begun their own efforts to share the Good News with others. Missionary disciples understand that they have a mission to accomplish.

Some parishes are using re-evangelization programs that target the baptized, those already familiar with Catholic culture and language. Many have had some success in reenergizing their parishes as lukewarm parishioners have turned into missionary disciples. When that has happened with enough parishioners to be noticeable, a parish is ready to ratchet up evangelism efforts to include lapsed Catholics, the unbaptized, and the unchurched, as well as those looking for the fullness of the faith that they can find only in the Catholic Church.

A parish can't get stuck at the re-evangelizing stage forever. If parishioners aren't turning into dynamic Catholics, then the program or process probably needs to be reexamined. Maybe try something else. If it *is* working, then a parish will gradually become the warm and welcoming place where you can begin to invite outsiders. At that point, the parish needs to shift gears to start casting a wider net with their evangelism efforts, and they need to help parishioners learn how to be part of those and other evangelism efforts.

At my parish, the Alpha course has been the tool we use both for re-evangelizing and broader evangelism efforts outside the parish. It works on a number of levels. First, it challenges practicing Catholics with the clear message of the Gospel and the necessity of having a relationship with Jesus Christ. Those trained to be hosts and helpers for Alpha courses learn how to be warm and welcoming, as well as how to interact non-judgmentally with those who might be at the very early stages of investigating Christianity. Alpha then provides an easy evangelization tool for parishioners to use as they invite friends, families, coworkers, and acquaintances to attend Alpha with them. There are a few other programs that share the goals of Alpha, but we judged it the most affordable and highest quality program available at this time.

Casting a Wider Net

The current culture is producing increasing numbers of unchurched and unbaptized people who have had little to no exposure to the Gospel. These people usually have very foundational questions about whether or not God exists, whether or not this God cares about people, whether this God can hear and answer prayers, and much more. They might know little or nothing about Jesus. It wasn't always this way in the United States.

In fact, it was quite different during the settlement of America and the founding of our country, and even up into the twentieth century. Christianity was a common denominator for most of the population. People were frequently exposed to the proclamation of the Gospel, whether or not they accepted it for themselves. Diligent pastors, camp meeting preachers, and celebrity evangelists presented the Gospel from a Protestant point of view. Catholics immigrated to the United States bringing their religious heritage and culture with them. However, Catholics rarely exhibited the evangelistic zeal shown by Protestants, most likely because priests and parishes already had their hands full caring for the souls that were already part of the Catholic culture.

The culture has changed radically over the past half-century or more. While Catholics do still immigrate to the United States and bring along their faith, their children too often abandon it. The secular culture pervading the media, schools, the arts, sports, and most everything else speaks louder and more persuasively than do parents, grandparents, and the Church. Additionally, broken families, unmarried parents, unconventional families, and other fallout from the sexual revolution have drastically weakened family structures so that homes rarely function as domestic churches.[1]

With some rare exceptions, we no longer live in a Christian culture. People might never be exposed to the message

---

[1]   "The Christian home is the place where children receive the first proclamation of the faith. For this reason, the family home is rightly called 'the domestic church,' a community of grace and prayer, a school of human virtues and of Christian charity" (*Catechism of the Catholic Church* 1666).

of the Gospel, and even if they hear it, that message often fights a losing battle with the much louder and more seductive message of our secular, materialist culture.

This has changed the landscape dramatically in terms of the task of evangelism. People rarely come to a church of their own accord, whatever the denomination. They have to be invited and brought in by others. They need to be evangelized outside the church. That means evangelization can no longer be left to the professionals on staff at the church. The laity have to become evangelists, reaching out to those they encounter and helping them come to know Jesus.

"But I can't do that!" you might be saying.

This is a hard sale. Most Catholics are full of excuses when it comes to evangelism. They say, "I don't know how to do that," while meaning, "There's no way I'm going to do that!" They have the idea that evangelism has to be an in-your-face, uncomfortable confrontation with others.

I want you to know that the best evangelism rarely happens with that approach. I believe that there are very natural and relational approaches to evangelism that anyone can use.

Generally, there is a lot of groundwork to do before someone is ready for spiritual conversion. The encouraging thing you need to know is that the process can be relatively easy and natural because the most important things you bring to the table are a love for the other person, a concern for their spiritual well-being, and a willingness to listen and invest time and friendship. This is a one-on-one investment. While I believe that these are the most important attributes you must have, knowledge is still important. You must have thought through your own faith to the extent that you can explain why you believe in God and why you are Catholic. As St. Peter tells us in his first epistle: "Always be ready to give an explanation to anyone who asks you for a reason for your hope" (1 Pt 3:15).

While we do not need to be expert apologists, we should be learning how to respond to the typical questions that arise. We should be continually growing in our knowledge of the Faith and of Scripture so that we are prepared to answer questions.

It's Not All About You

Before concluding this chapter, it's important to point out that ultimately the conversion process is the work of the Holy Spirit. We cannot take credit for it, and we cannot take the blame when it does not happen. The Holy Spirit works in the hearts of individuals at his own pace and through His often-unusual means. Think of the story of Philip and the Ethiopian eunuch in the eighth chapter of the book of Acts.

This story took place in the early years of the Church after Jesus had left his apostles and disciples to carry on his mission. Philip, one of Jesus's disciples, was told by an angel to head south on the road from Jerusalem toward Gaza. An Ethiopian eunuch, who happened to be a high court official of Queen Candace of Ethiopia, was traveling on the same road, but in a chariot. He had come to Jerusalem to worship as the story tells it, so he must have either been a Jew or converted to Judaism. Philip was somewhere behind the chariot when the Holy Spirit spoke to him and told him to go catch up with the chariot.

Philip ran up to the chariot and heard the eunuch reading prophecies about the suffering messiah from the book of Isaiah. Philip asked him if he understood what he was reading. The eunuch responded, "How can I, unless someone instructs me?" He then invited Philip to join him in the chariot and explain it to him. After hearing Philip's explanation of Jesus's fulfillment of these prophecies and of the message of salvation, the eunuch asked to be baptized immediately. They stopped by water that was conveniently nearby, and Philip baptized him (Acts 8:26–40).

Philip had no plan and no prior knowledge of what was going to happen other than that an angel told him to set out on a particular road. While there are some amazing supernatural elements in this story, the heart of the story is Philip being used by God to bring the good news of salvation to the eunuch. Philip made himself available, and God used him. Philip found himself in this extraordinary situation, but he grabbed the opportunity to ask a leading question. The eunuch was already spiritually seeking, and the Holy Spirit had already prepared his heart to hear and accept the Gospel.

> "We're all called—every one of us—to bring the Gospel to all those we encounter. We can't confine the love of God to our family, our parish, or our particular culture."[B]

I have found that this is often the case. The Holy Spirit has been working in someone's heart and orchestrates life circumstances to prepare him or her. A person is already opening up to God interiorly, even though he or she has said nothing to anyone else. Then God brings someone like you into the situation and the topic of God or faith arises. Do we capitalize on the moment like Phillip, or do we squirm our way out of the situation?

One of my goals in this book is to help prepare you to capitalize on those moments by cooperating with the work of the Holy Spirit. You don't have to be an expert apologist with all of the answers. You don't have to memorize a four-step plan to follow. You just have to be willing to trust the work that God is doing and love others enough to risk your own personal discomfort.

Discussion Questions

1. Where do you place evangelism in your list of spiritual priorities?

2. What impression do you think an outsider would get of the enthusiasm and engagement of the members of your parish at a typical weekend Mass?

3. Would you consider yourself a "dynamic Catholic," exhibiting the traits of prayer, study, generosity, and evangelism? In which of these areas are you weakest?

4. What evidence do you see of the erosion of Catholic culture and beliefs?

5. Have you ever invited a non-Catholic to come to Mass or some other Catholic event? How did it go?

CHAPTER 2

DON'T ASSUME ANYTHING

*Heavenly Father, please help us approach evangelistic
opportunities with a non-judgmental attitude. Help us to
first understand others rather than try to correct or admonish
them. May your Holy Spirit guide us in Jesus's name. Amen.*

I was listening to a podcast by Warren Cole Smith, Vice
President of the Colson Center for Christian Worldview,
as he interviewed Michael Cromartie, Vice President of the
Washington-based think-tank the Ethics and Public Policy
Center. One of Cromartie's most significant responsibili-
ties was to try to educate major media reporters about the
world of evangelical Christians. Cromartie mentioned that
these reporters, most of whom were very highly educated
and well-known, sometimes posed questions that caught
him by surprise because of the ignorance they revealed in
regard to religion. He mentioned a particular conversation
with a woman regarding the Southern Baptist Convention
and their position on marriage and the roles of men and
women. Cromartie started to explain, mentioning the book
of Ephesians as a source for Southern Baptist beliefs. She

interrupted him with, "Stop right there. What was that book you just mentioned? Who's the author? Who's the publisher?" Cromartie had to back up from the original questions to give her a primer on the contents of the Bible, starting from ground zero.[c]

The woman, seemingly, had no exposure at all to the Bible, even though it is the most popular book in all of history and was a major influence in the development of our civilization. Biblical illiteracy has become increasingly common. In our postmodern culture, many people have little to no exposure to the message of the Gospel, might have never set foot in a Christian church, and are totally ignorant regarding what the Bible says.

When it comes to evangelization, it's not safe to assume anything. The Pew Research Center's "Religious Landscape Study" from 2014 reported among young adults (ages 18 to 29), only 42 percent are either absolutely certain or fairly certain about their belief in God. If you spend most of your time with older people, you might have missed this loss of faith in younger generations. Consequently, if you get into a discussion touching on faith issues with a young adult, you might want to start with questions that will help you first determine if they even believe in God, and if so, what type of god that might be.

But the problem is not only with young adults. Many unbelievers of all ages hide behind religious identifications. The "Religious Landscape Study" found that 9 percent of Catholics and mainline Protestants are either not certain whether or not they believe in God or don't believe in him.

This is incredibly important to understand. As philosopher William Lane Craig puts it:

> What is true of the universe and of the human race is also true of us as individuals. If God does not exist, then you are just a miscarriage of nature, thrust into a purposeless universe to live a purposeless life.
>
> So if God does not exist, that means that man and the universe exist to no purpose—since the end of everything is death—and that they came to be for no purpose, since they are only blind products of chance. In short, life is utterly without reason.
>
> Do you understand the gravity of the alternatives before us? For if God exists, then there is hope for man. But if God does not exist, then all we are left with is despair. Do you understand why the question of God's existence is so vital to man? As one writer has aptly put it, "If God is dead, then man is dead, too."

Craig sums it up:

> If God does not exist, then life is futile. If the God of the Bible does exist, then life is meaningful. Only the second of these two alternatives enables us to live happily and consistently. Therefore, it seems to me that even if the evidence for these two options were absolutely equal, a rational person ought to choose biblical Christianity. It seems to me positively irrational to prefer death, futility, and destruction to life, meaningfulness, and happiness. As Pascal said, we have nothing to lose and infinity to gain."[D]

Belief in God is certainly foundational, but you can't count on any consistency in what people believe even if they say they believe in God in a way that sounds orthodox. In response to a question about whether or not they believe in heaven, 13 percent of those who are absolutely certain about their belief in God either don't believe in heaven or don't know if they believe in heaven. A question about belief in the existence of hell gets even worse results. Among those who absolutely believe in God, 27 percent either reject the idea of hell or don't know whether or not it exists.

Contradictory thinking carries over into moral issues as well. Among those absolutely certain about their belief in God, 42 percent believe that abortion should be legal in all or most cases. These kinds of contradictions are rampant even among regular church attendees.[E]

We cannot assume much of anything about the beliefs of the person we are talking to unless we first invest some time getting to know more about them and what they believe. I cannot overstate how important this is. You need to get to know the person you are talking to before trying to get into discussions regarding spirituality and religion. Even your own family members might surprise you with surprisingly unorthodox answers if you take the time to really find out what they believe.

I've found that evangelizing practicing Catholics is generally much easier than evangelizing the unchurched. If someone has been attending church yet has never had a personal relationship with Jesus, it seems like we're just "filling in the blanks" for them. Suddenly everything they have been doing by habit and obligation starts to make sense. They start to develop an intimate, more-conversational prayer life, and God becomes real and personal to them.

Evangelizing lapsed Catholics might range from easy to impossible. Much depends upon why they quit coming to the Catholic Church. Their reasons might relate to emotional trauma from a particular person or event; parents divorcing during their childhood; too many interactions with Catholics who behaved badly; sexual issues such as contraception, abortion, or homosexuality; marriage issues; other lifestyle issues (e.g., a preference to spend time partying rather than attending church or living a Christian lifestyle); and maybe even theology.

Evangelizing those from other faiths—introducing them to the fullness of the Christian faith that is found only in the Catholic Church—is entirely different. *Evangelization* isn't even the right word to use if we're talking about a change from Protestant to Catholic since many Protestants are already familiar with the Gospel and have a relationship with Jesus. We use the word *conversion*, but that word doesn't usually fit either since these situations are usually not a total about-face but rather a deeper movement into the truth of Christianity and acceptance of the authority and teaching of the Catholic Church.

While some Protestants become Catholics because of marriage or other relationships, many seem to convert for theological reasons. This is especially true with Protestants who are well-versed in Scripture. Marshall Fritz, a very intellectual Catholic, made the observation that Catholics with little knowledge of their faith (and who might never have heard a clear proclamation of the Gospel message) shift easily toward Protestant churches, while there is little movement in the opposite direction. Protestants with little knowledge of their faith much less frequently convert to Catholicism. But among the theologically well-educated, movement is in the opposite direction. You might have noticed that many Protestant pastors-have become Catholic for theological reasons, yet there is minimal opposite movement toward Protestantism among Catholic pastors and leaders who are knowledgeable about their faith. Marshall's diagram shows what this looks like. (From a personal conversation with the author.)

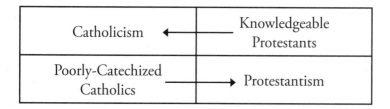

Catholicism ←	Knowledgeable Protestants
Poorly-Catechized Catholics →	Protestantism

Evangelism efforts with those outside the Christian realm are another matter. In our postmodern society, the barriers are more formidable and the process usually takes longer than you might expect because faith topics have been driven out of the public square—out of most of our schools, out of the workplace, out of the media, and out of even many family get-togethers. A shared, cultural familiarity with the Bible and basic tenets of the Nicene Creed has not been passed on to the last few generations. So there is often much groundwork to do before someone comes to faith in Jesus, and even more before they become Catholic.

Discussion Questions

1. Have you encountered surprising instances of religious or biblical illiteracy in others or in yourself?

2. Have you ever found fellow Catholics to be inconsistent in their beliefs? Have you personally struggled with conflicting beliefs?

3. What do you think of Marshall Fritz's diagram regarding conversions to and from Catholicism?

4. Have you ever tried to discuss faith with someone who did not believe in God? What happened?

CHAPTER 3

THRESHOLDS

God our Father, we ask for discernment as we talk with
others so that we can be aware of their progress on the
spiritual journey. Give us insight as to how best to help
them come to know you. We pray this in the name of the
Father and of the Son and of the Holy Spirit. Amen.

People rarely have dramatic and immediate conversion
experiences such as that of St. Paul in the book of Acts.
More commonly, the process takes quite a long time. Sometimes we encounter a person when he has already been
pondering spiritual questions for quite some time, and we
happen to talk with him at a point where he is ready to start
voicing questions after months of quiet thought or investigation. Other times, we might be planting seeds at the
very beginning of the process, seeds that might give him the
impetus to start considering his spiritual status.

In their book *I Once Was Lost*, Don Everts and Doug
Schaupp describe how they arrived at the idea of spiritual thresholds as a tool for those who hope to help others
become disciples of Christ.

Through numerous discussions with those who had recently become Christians, they realized that the conversion process often took months or even years. While they recognized that there are no guarantees that someone who starts to show interest in Christianity will eventually convert, Everts and Schaupp observed that there was a progression to the process that was common in most cases. They identified this progression as a series of *five thresholds*. These thresholds are like levels through which those on the path of conversion need to pass, generally in sequence. Perhaps it helps to think of it like the various levels of a Super Mario Brothers™ Nintendo game. The five thresholds as described by Everts and Schaupp are:

- trust,

- curiosity,

- openness to change,

- serious seeking,

- and becoming an intentional disciple.[F]

In *Everyday Evangelism*, I want to apply these thresholds to not only those moving from unbelief into a relationship with Jesus but also those with some belief and little practice, or those moving from Protestantism to Catholicism.

Members of yet another group—practicing Catholics who have no personal relationship with Jesus—usually follow a different progression. These Catholics usually already trust the Church and those representing her and are already trying to do the right thing. Sadly, they might have never been confronted with a clear proclamation of the Gospel and the call to personal conversion. When they finally hear it, they generally jump in at the second, third, or even fourth threshold, depending upon many factors.

The Holy Spirit Is Responsible

Everts and Schaupp point out that people sometimes stagnate at one threshold or revert to a lower threshold. This brings up one of the most important points we need to grasp when it comes to evangelism. Ultimately, conversion is the work of the Holy Spirit. We are privileged to participate in the process by helping others on their journey, but we can never take credit for bringing someone into the kingdom of God. The Holy Spirit works within each person in his time and through avenues of which we might never be aware.

People often begin down the path, building up trust, becoming curious, and even becoming open to hearing the Gospel and learning about the Faith. But recall the parable of the seeds in Matthew 13. Some seed lands on the path and birds quickly eat it. Some seed falls on rocky ground where it can't develop proper roots, sprouting up only to wither away quickly. Some seed lands among thorny weeds, sprouting but gradually choked out by weeds. Then some of the seed lands in rich soil where it takes root and grows into healthy plants.

We might have the opportunity to plant spiritual seeds. We can provide information, encouragement, prayer, and otherwise help spiritual seed take root and grow in others. But we don't control the ground of their lives or the care the seed receives. In other words, we don't get to control the outcome.

Just because we can't control the outcome, we don't have an excuse not to try. God wants to use us to bring others into a relationship with him. We need to be as openhearted and encouraging as possible to build at least that first threshold of trust with people so that they can turn to us for assistance and encouragement on their spiritual journey. That journey might move in a direct path at a fast pace, or it might be a meandering path with detours and pitfalls—a journey that takes years. They might abandon the path for a year or two, or they might seem to be abandoning it forever. Wherever people are in their journey, it helps if we can recognize which thresholds they have crossed and support and encourage them appropriately.

I highly encourage you to read *I Once Was Lost* for an in-depth exploration of the thresholds, but I'm including my own interpretation and application of the thresholds here so that you can begin to identify where people might be on their spiritual journey and learn how to interact with them most effectively at each level.

The First Threshold: Trust

Have you ever participated in a small group where even at the first session people are expected to open up and share personal experiences and feelings with a group of strangers? Many people clam up or talk only about superficial things because they don't know these people, much less trust them. This is a normal reaction, and probably a healthy one. It's generally not a good idea to share too much with someone you've just met for the first time, much less an entire group of new acquaintances. If enough time is allowed in these small groups to get to know one another with safe questions, it might take only one or two sessions before people feel safe getting into more personal discussions. The same dynamic generally applies to one-on-one conversations with new acquaintances, although I've had some amazingly personal conversations with people I have just met. Still, that's the exception rather than the rule.

We develop trust as we interact with and get to know another person. Or perhaps we don't develop trust and the relationship goes nowhere. Think of the street corner evangelist who attempts to convert people without bothering to get to know them at all. The likelihood of that approach being successful is very low.

I think the concept of "friendship evangelism" makes a lot more sense. I first heard about the idea of friendship evangelism in Matthew Kelly's book *Rediscover Catholicism*. He suggests purposely choosing someone you might already know or maybe an acquaintance, someone with whom you would love to share God's love. Kelly provides a specific plan for friendship evangelism. In simplified form, it means that you will pray for that person on your own while trying to build a genuine friendship with them if it doesn't already exist. After you've done this for six months, you can invite them to an event at your parish or otherwise try to introduce them to the world of your faith. Whether or not you follow Kelly's step-by-step plan as he explains it in his book, friendship is the starting place to build trust.

Over time, your faith should come up in at least a few conversations. You might have to bring it up, perhaps sharing about something exciting that God has done in your life or a personal concern about which you are praying. You are giving this friend a glimpse into your own life of faith and how you live it out.

You have to be careful about your own motivation. Yes, you want to bring this person into a relationship with Jesus. But your motive has to be your love for this person and your desire for them to "the best version of themselves," as Matthew Kelly puts it. It's not about counting coup with conversion scalps.

I have pursued forms of friendship evangelism with a few people that have proved fruitful over time. But, speaking from experience, you won't always get the results you want.

I've put years into one relationship with a friend, and she occasionally shifts into the curious stage but then backs down to trust. We have discussed praying about things, but her belief in God is shallow. I don't know if she'll ever make it even to a serious curiosity. Still, I continue to nurture the relationship. She, like many other people, might reach a point where she's ready to take the next step, and she'll know that I'm available for her whenever and if ever that happens. Sadly, those opportunities too often arrive only when tragedy strikes.

If you befriend someone like this, they might even reach the curiosity or openness threshold, but then they might back off from any spiritual discussion at all. Events in their lives might derail them. They might marry a non-believer and totally lose interest in faith issues because their new spouse has no interest and they don't want to rock the boat. They might go another spiritual direction, perhaps deciding to join a New Age church because it looks interesting or investigating Mormonism because their missionaries are so nice. Whatever happens, if you have developed a genuine friendship, you will continue to be their friend, even if they show no interest in pursuing Christianity.

Fallen Away Catholics

Those who are already baptized Catholics, yet aren't practicing the Faith, often go through a progression very similar to that of unbaptized Christians. If they were baptized but not raised in the Church, they don't even think of themselves as Catholic. You can approach them as you would most non-Christians.

However, Catholics who used to practice the Faith but have fallen away are another story. Sometimes, they've left the Church because they just never felt like it meant much. Maybe the kids' soccer games or sleeping in and then going to Sunday brunch seemed like more satisfying ways to spend their time. Maybe they never married, and they've found that spontaneous activities with friends frequently conflicted with attending Mass, so Mass attendance gradually declined. During their years attending church, they probably never developed a prayer life or a personal relationship with God. It's no surprise that they would choose relationships that seem more real and immediate rather than a church obligation.

This type of fallen away Catholic—one who has left

passively rather than by a conscious rejection of their faith—might be drawn back through some of the same avenues as non-Christians. However, they might have more defenses to overcome to gain their trust. After all, they will think that they have "been there and done that." There was nothing in it for them before, so why should that change? Our job might be to help these people get to know a God who is personal, a God who loves and cares for them, a God who wants a real relationship with them. Overcoming the trust threshold is your starting place with them.

Other fallen-away Catholics might be much more challenging. For one reason or another they don't trust the Church or the people in it. They either never had a personal relationship with Jesus or they have abandoned it for some reason. In such cases, it might be important to find out why. Maybe someone was turned away at a time of need. Maybe they or a relative suffered sexual abuse from a priest. Maybe their child was damaged by an incident at a Catholic school. Deep hurts, rejection, disillusionment, or actual harm might be the cause. These situations are much tougher to deal with. Healing probably needs to take place before they can trust. Tread lightly, listen carefully, and pray for wisdom in these cases. There are no magic answers for restoring a trust that has been abused.

Along the same line, Catholics who have left the Church over sexual issues often reject the Church as a way of defending their personal lifestyle choices. Cohabitation, irregular marriages, marriage outside the Church, and same-sex relationships make up the majority of these instances. The Church teaches against the errors of these lifestyle choices not to condemn anyone but to protect us from decisions that put our souls in jeopardy. If a person refuses to change their lifestyle, it will make their entry into the Church very difficult.

That being said, sometimes people find themselves in situations contrary to Church teaching without realizing it, and a wise pastor will work with those in such extenuating circumstances. For example, consider a non-Catholic woman who left her first husband because he was abusive. A few years later she remarries a good man. They have been married for twenty years when they jointly pursue an interest in becoming Catholic. In such a case, the Church would not encourage her to leave her second husband but would instead work with the couple to see if the woman's first marriage could be annulled and the present marriage blessed by the Church.

The Church will never waiver on standing up for truth, but she is also a beacon of Christ's mercy. If you or someone you know finds yourself in a difficult situation, I find that it's worth encouraging them to talk to a priest—one that you know is trustworthy with these delicate situations—to see if the Church can help them.

Bringing Protestants to the Trust Threshold

Reaching the trust threshold for a Bible-believing Protestant—that is, getting them to even trust the Catholic Church as a viable option—is frequently an entirely different process.

Most sincere Protestants have heard the Gospel and know

that they need a relationship with Jesus. They will claim that they have a personal relationship with Jesus—after all, this is one of the areas in which they take pride in comparison to Catholics, and maybe with good reason. Those people who form the small percentage of Protestants who do *not* have a relationship with Jesus can be addressed as nominal Christians who still need to receive the Gospel.

Most Protestants have an initial barrier to overcome that tells them their faith—even with all of its competing and conflicting denominations—is correct and Catholicism is not. A Protestant can change their allegiance from a Baptist to a Reformed Presbyterian congregation without anyone batting an eye. But shifting to Catholicism can elicit reactions ranging from merely being startled all the way to anger. So your initial task to get them to the trust threshold is probably more theological than in most other situations. Protestants are likely to raise issues about prayer to Mary and the saints, the Church hierarchy, the pope, salvation by works, and confession to a priest. Of course, they might raise other issues such as repeated prayers in the Rosary, the abuse scandals, or other peripheral concerns. Protestants will occasionally raise the issue of Catholic belief in the Real Presence of Jesus in the Eucharist, but many of them realize that there's no consensus on this issue within Protestantism on which they can take a stand.

Should We Even Be Trying to Convert Protestants to Catholicism?

I have many Protestant friends who are very strong in their faith. Many of them live lives that are much stronger witnesses to the truth of Christianity than are the lives of most Catholics. I have to believe that they are on their way to heaven. Even so, I want to share with them the fullness of the Christian life available through the Catholic Church.

They are missing out on the vehicles of God's grace, the sacraments, and particularly the Eucharist. I want all of God's grace for them!

If we love our Protestant brothers and sisters, we should want them to experience all that God has for them. We should want to share with them something more, something deeper, that they will find only in the Catholic faith.

Once in a while, a Protestant will raise a challenge against the Catholic Church, such as those I have mentioned, and it seems like there is no context for it. It can be hard to determine what prompted the question. Do they truly want an answer to the question? Do they simply intend to attack Catholicism? Is there another underlying issue driving them, such as a Catholic parent who deserted the family? In these cases, the best response might be, "Why do you ask?" At that point, the conversation might take an unexpected turn in a totally unrelated direction.

Still, many Protestants have serious misgivings about Catholicism. They typically have misconceptions about Catholic teaching that have arisen out of the centuries of rivalry that originated during the Reformation. In some cases, their misconceptions about Catholic teaching are based upon the words and actions of Catholics that do not accurately reflect or teach Church doctrine. Whatever the cause, misconceptions need to be addressed.

However, you don't build trust by arguing theological points. It has to start with the Catholic living an authentic Christian life. If you want to invite a Protestant to consider the Catholic Church, you are the walking advertisement. Are you convincing?

The more Bible literate a Catholic is, the better he or she will be able to converse with a Protestant. Protestant accusations that most Catholics don't read the Bible have sadly been true for too long, but that's changing with the many excellent Bible studies now offered in Catholic parishes. (At our parish, we often have three or four different Bible studies offered at a time, and I suspect there are many more parishes where Bible study has become very popular.) Clearly, theological knowledge and familiarity with the Bible are important if we hope to bring Protestants into the Catholic Church. I think the book *Catholic and Christian* by Alan Schreck is one of the most useful resources for educating yourself to be able to converse with Protestants. Schreck presents Catholic beliefs and explains them from a biblical perspective, something that is essential for Protestants. *Catholic and Christian* is valuable for educating Catholics themselves, but the conciliatory tone of the book makes it appropriate to give to Protestants to read for themselves.

Finally, Catholics need to be prepared to pray spontaneously with their Protestant friends. Nothing builds trust at the faith level like praying together for a particular intention. That doesn't mean praying a Hail Mary or the Our Father. Even though Protestants will occasionally pray the

Our Father (they more typically call it The Lord's Prayer), they would almost never do so when praying one-on-one. They will make up their prayer to fit the circumstances. There's nothing wrong with Catholics learning to do this. I will discuss this later in more detail since it is one of the most important tools in your evangelism toolbox. Shared prayer helps Protestants think of Catholics as fellow Christians rather than as those who might possibly be saved in spite of their Catholic faith.

Trust might be the most difficult barrier for some people to cross, especially for former Catholics. However, for many other people, the trust threshold is easily within reach through friendship evangelism.

Discussion Questions

1. Can you relate to the five thresholds in your own journey of deepening faith or conversion?

2. Have you recognized something like these thresholds in operation with a person you have tried to bring into faith or into a deeper practice of their faith?

3. Have you ever felt challenged by a biblically-literate Protestant who used Scripture to back up his or her beliefs?

4. What are some of the excuses or reasons you hear from fallen-away Catholics?

CHAPTER 4

SECOND THRESHOLD: CURIOSITY

Lord, we pray that you will inspire in those we hope to evangelize a spiritual curiosity that opens them to the possibility of a new or deeper relationship with you. Amen.

Have you ever had a close friend or relative ask you a spiritual question seemingly out of nowhere? It usually catches us by surprise if they've not shown any previous interest in spiritual matters.

Sometimes a person might reach the threshold of curiosity but be afraid to ask questions. Maybe they worry that people will assume too much and start pressuring them. Maybe they will think they are asking a dumb question. Maybe they don't even know whom or what to ask.

Events can happen that help trigger spiritual curiosity. We might be able to capitalize on those opportunities, making ourselves available for the person who has questions. For example, when a loved one dies, it can spark thoughts about the hereafter in even the staunchest atheists. So if your friend asks you what you think happens to us after we die, it's a clear sign that there is some curiosity at work.

Pope Francis's sometimes-controversial statements seem to prompt curiosity in non-Catholics in a way that happened far less frequently with other popes. If someone asks what you think about what the pope said, it could be a great opening for a conversation if you take care to confirm that the quote is accurate and has not been taken out of context. (This is not the time to start criticizing the pope.)

People can go through life seemingly complacent about spiritual matters. If pushed, they might say, "I don't know if there's a God, but it doesn't make any difference in my life." They can often get away with religious indifference until tragedy or an upheaval strikes.

While difficult circumstances might prompt curiosity, we need not wait for them to try to plant some spiritual seeds. We can attempt to stimulate curiosity in a few ways. The easiest and least threatening to others is for us to simply share what God is doing in our own lives. A friend or acquaintance will ask what I'm up to these days, and there is always something tied in with church or faith that gives me the opportunity to bring up the reality of faith in my life. Giving God credit for working out a tough situation or answering a prayer isn't likely to cause someone to convert on the spot, but it might prompt her to think about the possibility of prayer or the reality of God in her own life.

When I reverted from Protestantism to Catholicism, it was a big deal that caused a lot of gossip. I had been in the Protestant world most of my adult life, and I had been heavily involved in apologetics and teaching about worldviews.

When I realized I had to make this change to return to the Catholic Church in which I was originally baptized, I was obliged to inform conferences where I was contracted to speak during the next year. Many of them had statements of faith to which speakers had to adhere. Even most of those that didn't require a signed statement had an unspoken policy that Catholics weren't allowed to speak. Word of my changing religious allegiance spread like wildfire, and I was frequently confronted by people—by phone and in person—wanting to know why on earth I would do such a thing. This gave me an open door to explain the theological rationale for my determination that the Catholic Church had the fullness of the faith. It was my story, so people would usually listen without challenging me.

As I shared my story, I presented the questions that gradually funneled me back to the Catholic Church. I had to wrestle with questions such as: "How do we know that the canon of the New Testament is reliable?" "How were the books of the Bible selected?" and "What about those extra books in the Catholic Bible?" These questions had led me to even more foundational questions such as: "Did Jesus leave us with a way to sort out questions about basic doctrines such as how we are saved?" and "Did Jesus delegate authority to the Catholic Church that it has retained to this day?"

While those I was talking with already had strong faith in the Protestant tradition, some of them were initially closed to the possibility that Catholics could be Christians. Before the conversation, they had not the slightest curiosity as to whether or not the Catholic Church might be right about some things. After our conversation, some of them moved from believing that the Catholic Church was in apostasy to at least a mild curiosity, questioning some of what they had previously believed about it.

Some of those I discussed this with revealed that they had been struggling with some of the same questions themselves. They now felt freer to investigate Catholicism as a viable option. At least a few followed the path all the way into the Catholic Church.

My reversion to Catholicism gave me a natural platform, an invitation to tell my story. Sometimes sharing your own story of something God has done in your life or something that caused you to rethink your ideas about faith is entirely appropriate. Your story might help someone to see the reality of God's presence and care in a new or fresh way.

However, it is often better to be quiet about ourselves and instead spend more time listening to others and finding out what is going on in their lives. It has been almost twenty years since I came back to the Catholic Church, and I rarely share my reversion story these days. It seems more productive at this point to concentrate on listening to others and asking them questions about themselves.

We can be more direct with questions if we are cautious about it. If someone tells me they are struggling with a big decision, I might ask if they have prayed about it. I'm always surprised to hear a person I thought had little or no faith respond, "Yes. I've been praying about it." That kind of answer allows me to perhaps follow up with a question such as, "What has God been showing you?" This tells them that I believe that God answers prayer and that he listens to everyone who prays.

Maybe your friend won't admit to praying, but perhaps you can ask, "Would it be all right with you if we prayed about this situation right now?" Rarely will anyone turn down such a request. But then we had better be ready to pray a spontaneous prayer with them immediately! I have found that drawing people into prayer in this way without putting them on the spot is one of the most effective ways to help others grow in faith. Too often we say, "I'll pray for you," perhaps intending to pray on our own at a later time. But this usually sounds like a throw-away line just like, "Let's stay in touch," when both parties know it won't happen. It is far more effective to actually pray with someone then and there.

Maybe prayer is too much at this stage in your relationship. But perhaps you can raise questions about their spirituality in other ways. Asking questions that help them look at big worldview issues, such as the purpose of life, can spark spiritual curiosity in a roundabout way. If someone is considering a romantic relationship, you might ask a question such as, "Are you both on the same page about where you're going in life?" Or if he or she is a non-practicing Catholic and considering a relationship with someone who practices a non-Christian faith, "Have you thought about difficulties that might come up if you marry someone with those religious beliefs?"

A friend might be pondering a big decision that has to do with school or a career. This is another great opportunity to ask questions about what he wants his life to look like down the road. You might ask questions such as, "What's most important in your life and how does this decision affect that?" "Have you considered ethical issues that might arise from one choice or the other?" "How might that choice affect your friends and family?" And maybe even, "How do you think you would feel about yourself if you made one decision or the other?" Of course, you would phrase your questions in a more natural style that fits the conversation, but you get the idea.

I found myself in a discussion like this with a young woman who had recently broken up with her boyfriend. She said that she loved him, but she wasn't ready to make the commitment he was looking for at that point. I asked what she saw for her future and where she thought she was heading in life and gradually got to the really important question about her views regarding the purpose of life. While she didn't have an immediate answer, she pondered the question and eventually decided that a relationship with God was an important aspect of her life. Her conversion experience was a long, introspective process.

You might want to recommend audio or video recordings or books to those who are just reaching the curiosity stage. However, be cautious since it can be perceived as being pushy at this stage—a real turn off. C. S. Lewis's *Mere Christianity* might be a good starting place. While it's not a specifically Catholic book, it remains one of the best books for addressing some of the most important questions with which everyone should wrestle on their spiritual journey. Other C. S. Lewis books such as *The Great Divorce* or *The Screwtape Letters* might be equally helpful for those who enjoy more of a story approach.

A more modern book that might "speak" to a non-

Christian is *Something Other than God* by Jennifer Fulwiler. If a person has more of an intellectual approach, they might appreciate *The God Who Loves You: Love Divine, All Loves Excelling* by Peter Kreeft.

The Curiosity Threshold for Bible-Believing Protestants

For Bible-believing Protestants, the thresholds might be more tightly connected. In the process of coming to trust that Catholicism is a legitimate option, they will likely have already exhibited some curiosity. Generally, asking questions and learning more about the Church is essential before trust can be established. However, asking questions and sorting out theological and historical truth doesn't automatically put a Protestant on the path to Rome. Protestants have to become convinced that there is something more in the Catholic Church that they are missing within Protestantism. That something might be a sense of belonging and relationships, but more likely it will be theological and spiritual.

Unfortunately, most Protestant churches do a better job than Catholic parishes in welcoming and engaging those who show up on their doorstep. It's difficult to attend most Protestant churches without being warmly greeted and engaged in conversation. On the other hand, it is all too easy to attend a Mass without being greeted, much less engaged in any sort of conversation. While many Catholic parishes are making headway in becoming friendlier places, Protestants are not usually going to be drawn to Catholicism by an initial encounter with lots of friendly people.

One exception might be those Protestants coming in through the RCIA (Rite of Christian Initiation for Adults) process who are considering Catholicism because they plan to marry a Catholic. The RCIA process is generally a friendlier environment than your average weekend Mass.

The Alpha program, Discovering Christ (from ChristLife), Light of the World (from Light of the World Evangelization Ministries), and other programs now being implemented in many Catholic parishes are also exceptions. These programs are all about hospitality and being welcomed into a small group.

While hospitality and a warm welcome are critical components of a parish's evangelization efforts, more is needed. At our parish, a few of those who identified themselves as Protestants have gone through the Alpha course. It certainly broke down barriers in their thinking about Catholicism. Some of them have asked questions about the Catholic Church. But overall, it seems that most of those who are already church-attending Protestants at the beginning of Alpha rarely move beyond the trust and curiosity stages when it comes to the Catholic Church.

Moving beyond the trust and curiosity stages is where it becomes more important for Catholics to be familiar with Scripture and the theological issues dividing Catholics and Protestants. You don't need to know all of the answers, but there are common themes with which you should become familiar. The conversion stories of Protestants who became Catholics are a great place to start since they raise the same questions you are likely to encounter. Examples of books and videos featuring conversion stories are:

- *Born Fundamentalist, Born Again Catholic* by David Currie

- *By What Authority: An Evangelical Discovers Catholic Tradition* by Mark Shea

- *Crossing the Tiber* by Stephen Ray

- *The Protestant's Dilemma: How the Reformation's Shocking Consequences Point to the Truth of Catholicism* by Devin Rose

- *Rome Sweet Home* by Scott Hahn

- "The Journey Home" television show hosted on EWTN by Marcus Grodi (Videos can be accessed for free at https://chnetwork.org/journey-home/ as well as on YouTube.)

- *Surprised by Truth,* edited by Patrick Madrid (There are three books in this series, each a compilation of stories written individually by converts. I recommend starting with the first book in the series.)

- Why I'm Catholic website: stories by Protestant converts at www.whyimcatholic.com/index.php/conversion-stories/content/8-protestant-converts

Catholics who are able to carry on a conversation about theological topics and Scripture often surprise Protestants. That alone can be enough to help them shift over the threshold into at least becoming more curious about the Catholic Church and perhaps reconsidering some of their misconceptions.

Discussion Questions

1. Have you had something happen in your spiritual journey that gave you a natural platform to share your story?

2. Have you ever tried praying spontaneously in person with someone struggling with an issue or event? How did it go?

3. Have you ever visited a Protestant church? What was that experience like in terms of their hospitality and welcome?

4. How well-equipped do you think you are to carry on a conversation about faith with a Protestant?

5. Are you already familiar with any of the recommended resources? How have they helped you or others?

CHAPTER 5

THIRD THRESHOLD:
OPENNESS TO NEW IDEAS

*Loving Father, in gratitude for your patience as you
guide us on our own spiritual journeys, we ask that
you enable us to encourage and guide others to seek
your love and presence in their lives. Amen.*

Everts and Schaupp identify openness to change as the
next threshold to be crossed. I find it easier to think
of this threshold as openness to new ideas since a person
crossing this threshold is not yet ready to actually change.
They are by no means ready to embrace the Catholic faith,
but they exhibit a more non-specific openness. To cross this
threshold, people need to be willing to consider that something might be missing in their lives. They might have missed
something important in regard to their spiritual understanding, or they might have to be willing to consider the possibility of disruptive changes both interiorly in their spiritual
life as well as exteriorly in their lifestyle and relationships.

This is not a point at which the couple living together

without benefit of marriage figures out that they need to get married. But perhaps they start thinking about life down the road, their desire for children, and other family life issues, including where God might fit into the picture. If the partners are not on the same page regarding the role of faith in their lives, it might turn into a flash point that can either destroy the relationship or push them over the threshold of openness to new ideas and change.

This might be the point at which a young adult considering various career choices begins to think about what direction his or her life is heading. Does the young man want the pressure of the high power career in finance? How much of a personal life can he have if he goes that direction? Or does the young woman considering a career that involves lots of travel worry that the job will make it very difficult to form a lasting relationship that might lead to marriage? Or it might be the point where an addict figures out that something has to change if he is going to survive. Will that change include beginning a relationship with God?

Big life questions sometimes come into view at this stage. Maybe someone is asking himself for the first time, "What is the purpose of life?"

Becoming open to change often means becoming vulnerable in some way. It might mean stepping out of one's comfort zone and encountering new people and new ideas. But it might also present the awful possibilities of losing friendships, a career, or something else of significant value in one's life. Many people balk at this step because they judge that the change is too difficult. In these situations, the best thing we can do is pray for them to have discernment, wisdom, and courage to follow God's call.

Aside from risking vulnerability, people might harbor serious questions that make them think that Christianity, and Catholicism in particular, could never be an option for them, no matter how curious they might be. They might have questions—valid or not—such as, "How can a good God allow so much evil?" or "Doesn't believing in Christianity mean you have to reject a belief in what science tells us?" or "Why would anyone become Catholic since the Church hates homosexuals?"

Questions like these are difficult to deal with. I have found help in books and videos, and I would recommend that you take time to read or watch sources that will help you deal with these stumbling-block questions.

Few of us are prepared with a plausible explanation for the problem of evil this side of heaven, but we can be prepared with thoughtful ideas on the question by learning from those who have thought deeply about it. Some great minds have wrestled with this question in particular. Peter Kreeft has an excellent article titled "The Problem of Suffering Reconsidered."[2] Apologist Jimmy Akin has created a DVD presentation published by Catholic Answers titled "The Problem of Evil." Two classic books by non-Catholics on the topic are C. S. Lewis's *The Problem of Pain* and Alvin Plantinga's *God, Freedom, and Evil*. And Doug Schaupp, co-author of *I Once Was Lost*, has a series of short video conversations where he

---

2   Peter Kreeft, "The Problem of Suffering Reconsidered," *Catholic Answers*, March 1, 2002, www.catholic.com/magazine/print-edition/the-problem-of-suffering-reconsidered.

role-plays ways that you might answer this and other questions (visit YouTube to find these).

While all these are great resources, it's important to also draw off your own experiences when contemplating a challenge of this sort. When people ask me, "How can a good God allow so much evil and suffering?" I share a way of thinking about this question that has been helpful for me. On a trip to Poland, I was able to visit Auschwitz, the Nazi concentration camp that is the epitome of cruelty, suffering, and evil. On that same trip, I discovered the art of one holocaust survivor who portrayed the evils of Auschwitz as he imagined it from God's point of view. One image he created shows hundreds of cadaverous people being held up above a weeping Christ hanging on the cross. Jesus was carrying the burden of all of that suffering, entering into it just as he does with all the painful situations man has created.

This problem of evil and suffering in the world is not the only common stumbling block for people's faith in God and understanding Church teaching. Today's world presents us with all sorts of difficult issues, but there are good people who can help walk us through them. For example:

- Doug Schaupp has video online answering, "Doesn't science contradict the Bible?" (visit YouTube to watch).

- Jason Evert tackles "Homosexuality, Gay Marriage, and Holiness" in a video segment found on You-Tube. This particular segment is from Ascension Press's course *YOU: Life, Love, and the Theology of the*

Body, a program for teens that addresses other topics like this that are of great concern to young people.

- Daniel Rodger has a great article answering the question "Is Christianity a Psychological Crutch?"[3]

- Amy Orr-Ewing provides a succinct response to the question "Don't All Religions Lead to God?"[4]

These are just a few examples of the wealth of information available to you, even on the most difficult questions. Simple online searches will allow you to find these and more.

Provoking Questions

While becoming open to change doesn't mean people are ready to actually make a change, we might be able to give them a nudge or two in that direction if we do it carefully.

If you realize that someone might be approaching this threshold, you can help by simply being available to talk through questions. Responding with good questions that provoke deeper thought about things can be very helpful, and perhaps it will lead them in the right direction.

Recommending help from others who have traveled a similar path is also useful. Alcoholics Anonymous and its sister organizations come to mind as a model of this. If we know someone is an alcoholic and they are reaching a threshold

---

[3]   Daniel Rodger, "Is Christianity a Psychological Crutch?" *bethinking*, accessed May 24, 2018, www.bethinking.org/is-christianity-true/is-christianity-a-psychological-crutch.

[4]   Amy Orr-Ewing, "Don't All Religions Lead to God?" *RZIM*, April 11, 2013, rzim.org/a-slice-of-infinity/dont-all-religions-lead-to-god/.

where they are likely to admit they have a problem, it could be the perfect time for them to attend an AA meeting. Similarly, if someone seems to be struggling with big life questions and might be reaching this third threshold of being open to change, it is especially important that they have opportunities to ask those questions and talk about spiritual issues with a person who will be open and non-judgmental.

Discussion Questions

1. Can you recall a vulnerable moment in your own life when you questioned your religious beliefs . . . or lack of them?

2. Have you experienced a critical turning point in your life in regard to faith?

3. Have you ever had a conversation with someone who seemed to be reaching this threshold? How did it go?

4. Have you ever been challenged with hard questions similar to those I've mentioned in this chapter? How did you respond?

CHAPTER 6

FOURTH THRESHOLD: SERIOUS SEEKING

Lord Jesus, we ask that you fill us, as well as those we evangelize, with a hunger for your truth. Help us be willing to sacrifice our own wishes and desires to follow in your footsteps. Amen.

Once someone has passed the third threshold and become open to change, they are ready to seriously explore faith questions. Non-Christians will have decided that they need to learn more or at least become more familiar with what Christianity is all about. At this point, inviting them to an evangelistic program such as Alpha or Discovering Christ is a fantastic way to help them form a relationship with Jesus and start to pray. The gentle, welcoming approach works especially well for those who need to develop Christian friendships and a sense of belonging before they would even consider joining a church of any denomination. Your parish's RCIA Inquiry program might also be a good starting point if it is not run like a classroom experience. RCIA

Inquiry is supposed to be for those who are not sure that they will ever become Catholic as well as for those who have already made the decision. It needs to be a place where inquirers can ask any question and be treated in a welcoming manner even if they come for only a few sessions. Some people do better in a one-on-one situation, and you might be the only one they trust as they work through their spiritual journey at this stage. To help guide them, you might have them begin by reading the Gospel of Mark because it's the briefest of the Gospels and is fairly easy to understand. You might read and discuss the Gospel one chapter or section of a chapter at a time.

If they are a reader, you might have them read and discuss good books like those mentioned earlier or others that are more topic-specific, such as:

- *Why Do Catholics Do That? A Guide to the Teachings and Practices of the Catholic Church* by Kevin Orlin Johnson PhD.

- *The Lamb's Supper* by Scott Hahn. This book helps readers appreciate the beauty of the Mass and the Eucharist.

This might also be a good time for conversion story videos such as the *The Journey Home* interviews available online that I previously mentioned. The video *Convinced* by Don Johnson also features conversion stories of well-educated converts who came to Catholicism from many different spiritual and atheistic backgrounds. *Convinced* is available through Don

Johnson Ministries (donjohnsonministries.org) and, as of 2018, through Formed.org.

They might also be ready to investigate Catholicism by delving into the *Catechism of the Catholic Church*. The *Catechism* will answer many questions that arise, but be sure to work with them at first to show them how to use it. The *Compendium of the Catechism of the Catholic Church* might be an even better choice since it presents the content of the *Catechism* in a more concise and easy-to-understand format.

Sometimes the one-on-one spiritual journey is driven by conversations rather than reading. I've had people at this stage ask questions such as, "What kind of God would make his Son die for us?" This is a great opening to discuss the nature of the Trinity and the fact that this is God actually giving *himself* rather than an entirely separate being.

As another example, I am often asked questions about Baptism. Some questions have to do with the purpose of Baptism and some are in regard to a prior baptism. Many people were baptized as infants (as Catholics or in another denomination) or they have been baptized in a Protestant denomination. As long as the Trinitarian formula, "In the name of the Father, and of the Son, and of the Holy Spirit," is used and they are sprinkled, dunked, or otherwise had contact with water, their baptism is probably valid. They do not need to get baptized again. People can be surprised by this. These questions are a great opportunity to talk about the nature of sacraments and the fact that they actually accomplish something. They are not merely symbolic. In the case of Baptism, once someone is baptized, they have been adopted into the family of God and original sin has been removed. This cannot be undone or redone. Of course, there is the sacrament of Reconciliation for the removal of sin after Baptism, but that can lead into yet another conversation.

With someone who is seriously seeking, we need to be willing to share our own stories from our spiritual journey if they are applicable, and we need to be able to engage in conversations about the Faith. Some questions might take us beyond where we have gone in our own questioning, but that's okay. And perhaps it's even better than okay if it helps us deepen our own spirituality and theological understanding.

You cannot predict what questions someone will ask unless you know a person well, and maybe not even then. There is no one resource that will be more helpful to you than a Bible and the *Catechism of the Catholic Church*. You should spend time becoming familiar with both to use them in these settings. Still, if you get stumped by a question, you can ask if you can have some time to make sure you give them a thorough and accurate answer. Then do some homework on that topic.

Serious seeking is not just about asking questions. For many people, the sense of belonging is more important than theological investigation. They want a spiritual community where they feel like they have friends, activities, and support when they face life's challenges. Because of this, it might be a good time to invite serious seekers to parish events that offer opportunities to get to know people. If you invite someone to a parish event, make sure that you take time to make introductions and help your guest feel comfortable.

Serious seekers might even be ready to attend Mass. However, I find that first encouraging someone to simply spend time with Jesus in the adoration chapel or in the church itself helps them start to feel comfortable in the environment. Accompanying them on their first visit is usually a good idea.

If someone has never attended a Mass, prepare them in advance with a brief explanation of what happens—we acknowledge our sinfulness by praying the Confiteor and/ or the Kyrie and asking for God's mercy and forgiveness; we praise God through the Gloria; we listen to the Word of God through the readings and homily; we offer our gifts to God in the Offertory; we celebrate the consecration and Holy Communion; and then we are dismissed.

Alert them in advance as to how the Sign of Peace is shared in your parish as well as what to do when you leave them to go to join the procession for Communion. This might also be a good time to spend time with them in the Gospel of John, chapter 6, for a discussion of the Eucharist, but that will depend upon the concerns and needs of each person.

The point is that you want to try to make them as comfortable as possible in this new setting.

Intellectuals Sometimes Seek Before Counting the Cost

Most people have to "count the cost" before they are willing to ask questions when those answers might disrupt their lives. While Everts and Schaupp consider this the normal order of progression—openness to change followed by serious seeking—I have found that people with an intellectual bent will sometimes explore important faith questions as an intellectual pursuit without first considering the personal cost. They are so oriented toward truth-seeking that they aren't in the habit of considering the repercussions of uncomfortable discoveries in advance.

These people might already be in the process of serious seeking when they discover the implications. They were not open to change when they started asking questions, perhaps because they expected to find more comfortable answers to their questions. But at some point in their questioning, they have to consider whether or not they are open to change. They might decide they are not.

Some stop exploring dangerous questions, but they can be left with serious cognitive dissonance since they now know something that doesn't align with their previous theological views. Others decide that it's worth following the truth wherever it leads and whatever the cost. In many of the conversion stories of Protestant pastors to Catholicism, I see this alternate pathway to conversion where serious seeking precedes openness to change. The point is that although there is a typical progression through these five thresholds, there will also be exceptions.

Discussion Questions

1. Have you ever worked one-on-one with someone at the serious-seeking stage? How did you handle that?

2. Have you ever shared a story of your own spiritual experiences, growth, or conversion?

3. Can you think of an experience of yours that might be suitable to share at this stage with someone?

4. Have you ever prepared a non-Catholic before they attended Mass with you? If yes, did it make a difference?

5. Do you know someone who has taken an intellectual approach to faith questions that seemed contrary to what you would normally expect?

CHAPTER 7

FIFTH THRESHOLD: BECOMING AN INTENTIONAL DISCIPLE

*In thanksgiving for your infinite love and mercy, we ask
that you inspire us with missionary zeal that will help
us draw others into a relationship with you. Amen.*

The final threshold is the point at which someone chooses
to become an intentional disciple. They are choosing to
follow Jesus. Church becomes an important factor at this
point. It's not just about a relationship with Jesus. It is also
about a person's relationship with Christ's Church.

Returning Catholics

For those who are already Catholic, becoming an intentional disciple generally means either practicing their faith
at a deeper level or reconnecting with the Church. Those
connecting at a deeper level generally are eager to learn more
about their faith. They will be looking for Bible studies and

other learning opportunities and are likely to also seek out opportunities to serve and be more involved. Parishes intent on the New Evangelization need to be prepared with these types of activities.

Those who need to reconnect with the Catholic Church after years away might find it more challenging. They will need to go to confession, but as I mentioned in the second chapter, they sometimes bring with them other issues— invalid marriages, sexual relationships outside of marriage, distrust of the Church, or other circumstances or attitudes that might prove to be significant hurdles to overcome before they can partake in the sacraments.

The reality is that in our modern culture, the rules of the Catholic Church regarding marriage and sexual relationships are commonly perceived as outdated and unnecessary restrictions on personal choice or self-actualization. Some people might make it through the fourth threshold, but they will either stall out at the fifth threshold or they might choose a different denomination that is less demanding in regard to their personal life.

These people reject Catholicism without understanding its high view of the dignity of each person. They might never have heard any teaching on the theology of the body and the beauty of sex in its proper place. They might have turned a blind eye to the disastrous results of the sexual revolution, especially the critical role that artificial contraception has played in contributing to marital infidelity and promiscuity as predicted by Pope Paul VI in his encyclical *Humanae Vitae*.

Sadly, to hold faithfully to Catholic teaching in these areas sometimes means having to watch people walk away. However, if we are prepared to discuss the reasons for Catholic teachings on sexual issues, we might be able to help draw people into an appreciation for the wisdom and beauty of those teachings. If you want to learn more yourself about these topics, *Humanae Vitae* is a great starting point. Christopher West has written very accessible books on the topic that are useful, especially *Theology of the Body for Beginners* and *Good News About Sex & Marriage (Revised Edition): Answers to Your Honest Questions about Catholic Teaching*.

I know that some of those reading this book will be working within their parish to promote evangelism. Catholic programs designed for the New Evangelization are often particularly good for helping people move past this fifth threshold. Many parishes have had great success with programs like:

- Amazing Parish (amazingparish.org)
- Be My Witness (a program of RENEW International at bemywitness.org)
- The Evangelical Catholic (www.evangelicalcatholic.org)
- Rebuilt (rebuiltparishassociation.com)
- Catholic Christian Outreach (cco.ca/resources/faith-studies-series/)

In my own parish, we have seen many lapsed Catholics return to the Church after participating in Alpha (alphausa.org/catholic/) even though that program has much broader goals.

Sherry Weddell's book *Forming Intentional Disciples* is a great resource to prepare those working with returning Catholics or for individuals who want to deepen their own relationship with Jesus and his Church.

Bringing Non-Catholics into the Catholic Church

Protestant churches generally have much lower barriers to membership than the Catholic Church. You can help someone develop a relationship with Jesus, but getting them to become Catholic is quite another endeavor. Many Protestants believe that all one needs to do to be saved is to recite the "Sinner's Prayer." There are no specific words for this prayer, but they essentially include three points: sorrow for sin and asking forgiveness, expressing faith in Jesus's death for our sins, and asking Jesus to come into our life. Here is one typical example from the Billy Graham Evangelistic Association:

"Dear God, I know that I'm a sinner, and I ask for Your forgiveness. I believe Jesus Christ is Your Son. I believe that He died for my sin and that you raised Him to life. I want to trust Him as my Savior and follow Him as Lord, from this day forward. Guide my life and help me to do your will. I pray this in the name of Jesus. Amen."[G]

While there's nothing wrong with this type of prayer in itself, it falls short of what Catholics as well as some Protestants and others would identify as essential elements for becoming a Christian. The clearest directive for how a person becomes a disciple of Jesus is in Scripture itself, where Jesus tells his disciples to "go therefore and make disciples of all the nations, baptizing them in the name of the Father and the Son and the Holy Spirit, teaching them to observe all that I commanded you" (Mt 28:19–20).

But, this too is an isolated verse. The entire process involves repentance, belief, commitment, and the sacrament of Baptism.

Most Protestants advocating the Sinner's Prayer method of evangelism believe in the idea of "once saved, always saved." This means that if a person prays the Sinner's Prayer with sincerity, he is saved no matter what he does with the rest of his life.

In contrast, the Catholic Church teaches that salvation is an ongoing process. We begin with the sacraments of initiation—Baptism, Confirmation, and the Eucharist—and continue to "work out our salvation" in "fear and trembling" (Phil 2:12). I like the summary of the Catholic view of salvation I have heard a number of times: "I was saved, I am being saved, and I will be saved." This clearly states the ongoing nature of salvation. We have to persevere till the end.

For Protestants, the most challenging goal is getting someone to pray the Sinner's Prayer. There might be a more involved process to become a voting member of a congregation that offers voting privileges, but almost anyone can attend a Protestant service and receive communion with no questions asked.

Catholics are much more focused on the ongoing nature of salvation and how we live out our faith. To that end, the Catholic Church requires that those who have reached the age of reason—about seven years old—be catechized before they can become Catholic. The Catholic Church wants to ensure that those entering the Church have some familiarity with the liturgical and sacramental nature of the Church as well as its basic doctrines. Of course, that preparatory period should also be used to insure that people have a personal relationship with Jesus and that they are developing an active prayer life.

Those who are unbaptized are supposed to go through RCIA, a process that should take at least one full liturgical year. Those already baptized in another Christian denomination also go through RCIA but as candidates for full initiation into the Church since they have already been initiated into Christianity itself through their baptism. This, too, is usually a lengthy process.

Not uncommonly, adults seeking to become Catholic bring with them marriage issues from past marriages and divorces, just like returning Catholics. Marriage issues need to be straightened out before they can be received into the Church. I have worked with people whose cases took three or more years! That is a long time to wait to enter the Catholic Church. So becoming Catholic is almost always a more complex and demanding process than becoming a Christian in Protestant denominations.

Protestant churches don't have these barriers. In today's culture, which highly prizes self-determination, the requirements of the Catholic Church seem to be a bridge too far for some people. They expect that their desire to become Catholic immediately should be the overriding driver of the process.

I have watched people walk away rather than go through the process. I do not want to be discouraging, but this is the reality of evangelism.

Social Barriers

Some people are much more intimidated by the social barriers to becoming Catholic. Picture what it must be like for the unchurched person who decides to check out Catholicism by attending Mass. Our initial reaction might be, "That's great!" After all, isn't Mass the most important and most visible of Catholic gatherings?

So this person who has never before stepped foot in a Catholic Church finds out where and when to show up for a Mass. Odds are, they won't be greeted and there won't be anyone available if they have questions about where they should sit or where the restrooms are located. Before Mass even begins, the visitor might notice that other people are doing this funny little bow or half-kneel when they enter pews. Is everyone supposed to do that? And which is it? Bowing or kneeling? And what about the hand motions they are making? Then as Mass begins, Catholic calisthenics seriously kick in: stand up, sit down, stand up, sit down, kneel, stand up, and on it goes. All through the Mass, people around them suddenly respond with obviously memorized responses, but the visitor has no idea what they are mumbling. How does anyone know what to say and when to say it? Should the visitor join in singing or is that not allowed? Those surrounding them aren't consistent in whether or not they sing, so how do you know? And what do they do when everyone else in their pew starts to line up for Communion? Talk about feeling lost in an alien culture!

The Alpha course has made us keenly aware of this problem. We've tried to address it by asking our Alpha hosts and helpers to offer to be "Mass buddies." If they know that someone in their group is not Catholic and has never been to Mass, or someone was raised Catholic but hasn't attended in so long that they are unfamiliar with what to do, the host or helper offers to meet up with them to attend Mass together. They should show them what to do and explain as much as is needed. We've also added a church tour for those participating in our Alpha course just so people feel comfortable walking into the church. They'll know what the holy water fonts are for, and they'll know something about bowing or genuflecting when they enter a pew. These few simple explanations help lower the discomfort level for those for whom Mass attendance is unfamiliar.

The RCIA Process

Some might point out that the RCIA process is a better entry point than Mass for a non-Catholic. It can be, but the idea of even signing up for something called the Rite of Christian Initiation for Adults might be intimidating. While the RCIA Inquiry period is supposed to be very open, some parishes offer Inquiry sessions just like a series of classes. People sign up and are expected to "graduate" into the catechumenate, ready to commit at the same time as their fellow travelers in the Inquiry group.

In my experience as director of RCIA at our parish for a decade, by the time people come to Inquiry, many of them have already been through at least some preparatory evangelization through other people or their own personal reading and research. But they bring with them different concerns. For example, one inquirer has a Protestant background and is wrestling with prayer to the saints and the role of Mary. Another inquirer has come to know Jesus, but has no idea why the Catholic Church is better than the Protestant church down the street. Yet another inquirer is marrying a Catholic and wants to become Catholic so that they are on the same page, but she is concerned that her Buddhist parents will be greatly offended if she gives up her former religious practices.

And then there is the inquirer who comes with a list of challenges and objections rather than a readiness to learn and grow. Others in the Inquiry session can easily be alienated by the person who is challenging Catholicism with accusations that the other inquirers had never even considered. Belligerent inquirers need to be taken seriously, but one-on-one conversations are a better venue for addressing their concerns.

While the Inquiry step of the RCIA process is intended to be communal rather than individual, this is a time when individual attention is critical. Inquirers need their questions addressed, whether within or outside the group setting. While some parishes are doing a terrific job with the Inquiry process, others treat it as just another catechetical course.

In our parish, we've expanded the Inquiry process to address the needs and schedules of those who might be considering becoming Catholic. There are weekly Inquiry sessions, but there is no set agenda for those sessions most of the time. Sessions begin by asking Inquirers what questions are on their minds. The session facilitator is usually prepared with material regarding a foundational topic if there are no questions. However, one inquirer might ask a question that prompts another to ask a question which leads to another and another, consuming the entire evening with what matters most to them. Granted, this approach works best if the group is relatively small. We've had occasions where the needs of the group were so diverse that we needed to split them for separate discussions.

We were also concerned about those who were not able to make the scheduled Inquiry sessions because of their work schedules. So we have volunteers who have worked one-on-one with them, meeting at times convenient for both parties.

The "Got Faith Questions" table that I described in the introduction also serves as an on-ramp for those who are not yet ready to come to an Inquiry session. There is no obligation to show up, but some have used the opportunity to come regularly and work through their questions about Catholicism.

The point is that in today's culture we might need to adapt our RCIA process so that it truly meets the needs of those who are considering becoming Catholic.

A More Gradual Path

One of the most important aspects of the five thresholds that we need to keep in mind is that people move through their spiritual journeys on their own schedules. Some people quickly come to a decision to become Catholic, while others take years.

Those who are investigating but have not yet committed are often in an awkward spot. This is another issue of which we became aware through the Alpha course. Someone might attend Alpha and decide they want a relationship with Jesus, but they might not yet be sure about what that entails. They are still investigating. On top of that, they might have no familiarity with the sacramental and liturgical life of the Church. They are in no way ready to slide right into Catholic rituals and prayers. They might have connected with their Alpha group, but they have not connected with the larger church. When Alpha ends, there might be no one keeping in touch with them or taking them under their wing to help lead them into discipleship.

This situation arises outside of Alpha as well. People become interested in investigating the Church, but they don't have anyone to guide them or answer questions.

Holy Trinity Brompton, the Anglican parish that developed Alpha in London, England, forms Connect groups. Many churches have copied that model. However, Catholic parishes, aware of the higher barriers faced by those considering becoming Catholic, are developing their own versions of Connect groups and other types of Alpha follow-ups.

In our parish, we decided to adopt a Discipleship Group model developed by Our Lady of Good Counsel parish in Plymouth, Michigan. Father John Ricardo, pastor of that parish, presented five foundational talks that explain what it means to become a disciple of Jesus Christ, the cost of discipleship, and how this is lived out. He has additional talks— available through YouTube—that can be used following these five sessions. The sessions are meant to operate like an initial evangelism program with social interaction and small group support being paramount. Groups will share food, watch a video, discuss questions, and pray for one another.

Our Discipleship Groups have each taken on their own

individual flavors. One group has gone deeper into the topic of prayer using the *Oremus* study from Ascension Press after Father Ricardo's first series of talks. Members of another group meet during the months between our twice-a-year Alpha courses, then they take a hiatus while they volunteer as hosts, helpers, or other assistants for each Alpha course. Another group has revisited the five foundational videos as they've drawn new members into their group.

The point is that our Discipleship Groups exist to help grow disciples by whatever path works best for each group. Discipleship Groups are relatively new for us, just over a year old, so we're still learning how they fulfill the needs of those in different places on their spiritual journey. But it does provide personal and social support along the path of discipleship that so many people need.

Finding the Right Path into the Church

The person trying to bring someone into the Catholic Church might not be in or near a parish offering options such as those I have described, and the RCIA process at their parish might not be the right option. Many evangelization efforts are new at some parishes and unheard of at others. That leaves the burden on the evangelizer to try to provide other options that gradually answer questions and explore the teachings and practice of the Catholic faith. I'll offer a few suggestions that might help in those situations.

- Usually, there will be one or more people at your parish who should be able to help answer questions or provide spiritual direction. This might be a priest or someone else dedicated to the religious life, but it might be a member of the laity. Enlist their help if it is appropriate and useful.

- Read useful books together. You might agree to read a chapter a week and discuss each one. Choose a book that is appropriate for the stage of the person's spiritual journey. Many books I've suggested in the different chapters might work for this.

- Watch videos and discuss them. Think broadly about possibilities. Some suggestions might be:

- "Journey Home" interviews where host Marcus Grodi chats with converts and reverts to Catholicism who have been in leadership roles.

- Theological debates: Watch a debate together and discuss it. You can find many on the internet, but screen them first to make sure they are appropriate. One dependable Catholic debater is Trent Horn. Check out some of his debates online. Another great debater, Tim Staples, has participated in a number of debates that you can easily find on YouTube.

- Stories of saints. Formed (formed.org) is a subscription website with a huge number of options, including videos on saints such as Mother Teresa, Padre Pio, Pope St. John Paul II, Saint Thérèse of Lisieux, and Maximilian Kolbe.

- Watch "Convinced," a program that interviews former Protestants and atheists who became Catholic.

Convinced is available through Don Johnson Ministries and through Formed.org.

- Current issues: Formed.org has a few great videos addressing current issues from a Catholic perspective that might be jumping off points for further discussion. Some examples: "Who Am I to Judge?: Responding to Relativism with Logic and Love," "Happiness," and the series "Marriage: Unique for a Reason."

Discussion Questions

1. Have you known someone who has wanted to become Catholic but was discouraged or put off entirely by what it required?

2. Do you feel competent to answer questions from a Protestant about the purposes of the sacraments? What do you find difficult to explain?

3. Have you personally felt a need for support and encouragement as you try to figure out how to be an intentional disciple? Have you received that support and encouragement? If so, in what way?

4. Does your parish offer anything outside the RCIA program to help bring people into the Church? If not, what do you think might work in your parish? Can you help make that happen?

5. Do you have any suggestions for working with people who are facing the final threshold of becoming an intentional disciple?

CHAPTER 8

WORLDVIEWS: GETTING TO CORE QUESTIONS

Lord God, creator of the universe, open our eyes to the wonders of your creation. Help us be always aware of your presence and care in all areas of life. Amen.

Catholic film producer, author, and talk show host Don Johnson created an excellent video course titled *Personal Evangelism* that we used with a group of about fifty participants at our parish. One of the key ideas Don presents is that when we get into evangelism-related discussions, we should avoid getting drawn off into the weeds with peripheral questions about topics such as the Church's teaching on homosexuality or abortion or the Church's restrictions about who is able to receive Holy Communion. He recommends, instead, redirecting the conversation to basic worldview questions such as "Does God exist?" "What is the nature of man?" or "What is the purpose of life?"

I noticed that many participants in the study were not familiar with the term *worldview*. So, of course, they also didn't know what those basic worldview questions might be. They certainly could not come up with them on their own.

I believe Johnson has identified a very important strategy that anyone involved in evangelism should use. However, for most Catholics, this first requires a more foundational explanation about worldviews.

The term *worldview* is used to describe how each of us looks at all areas of life based on our core beliefs. Our worldview is our set of lenses through which we view the world. Consider the person who looks at the world through rose-colored glasses in contrast to the person peering through gray-colored glasses. The one wearing rose-colored glasses will describe many things as having a warm, rosy tint, while the gray-lensed viewer will perceive colors around him as drab and dull.

Just as our visual landscape can be strongly influenced by the color of lenses, our worldview is formed by what we believe about the most important questions of life, questions such as:

- Can we know that anything is really true?

- Is there a supernatural realm or is matter all there is?

- Is there a god?

- If so, what type of god is he?

- If there is a god, how can we know anything about him?

- What is the nature of man?

- What is the purpose of life?

- What happens when we die?

Based on our answers to these fundamental questions, we tend to form beliefs and opinions about all areas of life—the nature of families, the purpose of work, the value of relationships, how we view the poor, the importance of telling the truth, the role of science, and even expressions of the fine arts. Maybe that sounds like a stretch to you, but consider this: C. S. Lewis commented, "I believe in Christianity as I believe that the Sun has risen, not only because I see it, but because by it I see everything else."[H]

Like Lewis, if we have a Christian worldview, we should interpret and make sense of the rest of life through that lens. For example, because I believe in a God who has revealed himself to us and who has given us moral directives such as love God and love your neighbor (Mt 22:37–39), I also believe that I should be patient with the person driving in front of me who is holding up traffic, or I should take the time to listen graciously to my elderly grandfather's story for the umpteenth time, or I should give to charities that serve the poor. If I do not believe in God or that he wants me to love my neighbor, then I can easily find reasons not to do any of these things unless I think I can get something for myself out of it.

It helps to understand a person's underlying worldview when we are going to have a conversation about faith, God, or religion. Otherwise, the conversation can get derailed in all sorts of useless directions.

Here is a common example of where the conversation goes wrong. A mother is concerned about her adult son who has not gone to Mass for years. She assumes that he is still a believing Catholic since he was raised that way. So she asks him if he has gone to confession lately, which he perceives as nagging. In reality, his faith was half-formed and never truly something he claimed for himself. He's not sure whether he even believes in God. So going to confession isn't even on his radar of things he might consider doing. But his mother hasn't taken the time to find out what he actually believes or why. In a sense, she is putting the cart before the horse, and her question only alienates him further.

Less common is the situation where someone challenges you about the Catholic Church with something like, "Catholics can't think for themselves. They can only do what the pope tells them." It's all too easy to get defensive and respond with something like, "That's not true. I think for myself." But that just devolves into an argument that leads nowhere: "No you don't." "Yes, I do." "No you don't.". . .

It might be more useful to turn it around and ask the challenger, "Why do you think that's true?" In my experience, there's usually one hot-button issue, such as abortion or same-sex marriage, that is behind the question. But that doesn't mean that you should get into a debate about abortion or same-sex marriage either. Those are still positions that are derived from the person's worldview.

You might start peeling back the layers by continuing to ask "why questions" to find out whether or not they believe in God, what they believe about the nature of man, and what they believe about standards of right and wrong.

Obviously, people answer worldview questions such as those I've listed above in different ways. Many take for granted something that another person vehemently denies. For example, while there are some vociferous atheists who get lots of media attention, there are many more people who have always believed in some sort of god, even if they have not spent time trying to figure out what type of god it might be. Your discussion with an atheist might be directed toward discovering the roots of that atheism—an abusive father, scientism (a belief that only things that can be proven by science are real), a bad experience with a church, et cetera. In my experience, few people are absolutely convinced of their atheism, and there's always a story as to why they have come to that belief.

More often, you will encounter a person who at least vaguely believes in a god of some sort. A discussion with that person can move pretty quickly past the question of whether or not there is a god to figure out what sort of god this person has in mind. That's a very different conversation than one with someone who insists there is no god at all. You might ask questions such as, "Do you pray?" and "Does God answer your prayers?" to find out whether or not the god they believe in is a personal God who cares for them. You might ask questions to try to discover how they came to believe in this god.

People who have spent time pondering these deep worldview questions often arrive at a worldview that is at least somewhat coherent—what they say they believe generally fits together logically to some extent. However, many people—probably the majority—absorb their worldview from the surrounding culture, family, and friends without seriously examining it. They tend to believe whatever those they hang around with believe.

Often worldviews cobbled together in this fashion are

incoherent, and different aspects of what a person says they believe contradict one another. A person who claims to be a Catholic also says that she believes in reincarnation, or a Buddhist says he believes in heaven. (Reincarnation has no place in Catholic theology, nor does heaven fit into a Buddhist worldview.) A fortunate few who absorb their worldview from the people surrounding them have been blessed with an accurate and faithfully-Catholic worldview. But this is rarely the case.

The incoherence of worldviews shows up frequently in public discourse. It's not uncommon to hear someone say, "No one can know for certain what is true or not." They don't realize that they have just contradicted themselves by making a definitive statement in regard to truth. They are essentially saying, "I am certain that it is true that no one can know what is true." More visible instances of worldview incoherence can be seen with political figures, especially self-proclaimed Catholics who openly support issues clearly in opposition to Church teaching such as abortion, euthanasia, and same-sex marriage.

Within the Catholic world, worldview contradictions are rampant when it comes to faith issues. The 2014 Religious Landscape Study from the Pew Research Center found that only 50 percent of those who call themselves Catholic are either fairly certain or absolutely certain that they believe in God. That leaves the other 50 percent unsure about God's existence or certain that he doesn't exist.[1]

Wouldn't you expect that if someone claims to belong to the Catholic faith they would, at a minimum, believe that God exists? Yet too many Catholics have been baptized into the Catholic Church and maybe even raised in the Church, but their faith (or lack of faith) is often largely unexamined. They still think of themselves as Catholic, not realizing that the essentials of Catholic identity include the first line of the Nicene Creed: "I believe in God, the Father almighty."

Perhaps this disconnect helps explain why another Pew Research Center study found that 48 percent of Catholics in the United States think that unmarried parents living together is "acceptable and as good as any other arrangement for raising children" and that a same-sex couple cohabiting is "acceptable and as good as any other way of life."[J]

Inconsistent thinking is rampant, and not just among Catholics and politicians. This is a reflection of our relativistic culture that says there is no truth we can know for certain. It's all up to the individual and what they think. People often say, "That might be true for you, but it isn't for me."

As you might have figured out, it is important for us to think through our own worldview before attempting worldview conversations with others. We need to answer questions such as those I posed at the beginning of this chapter for ourselves. We need to challenge our own thinking and beliefs by asking, "Is this truly what I believe?" and "Does this make sense?" Taking it further for those of us who wish to live as faithful Catholics, we need to compare our beliefs with the teaching of the Church. We need to ask ourselves questions such as whether or not we truly believe in the Incarnation. Do we believe that Jesus established a Church? Do we believe that Jesus actually gave us his Body and Blood through the Eucharist?

If you are not sure what we need to believe as faithful

Catholics, you can start with the Nicene Creed for our basic profession of faith. However, there are other foundational teachings of the Catholic Church which we must believe, teachings regarding the sacraments, apostolic succession, the priesthood, the communion of saints, the role of Mary, and other important topics. The *Catechism of the Catholic Church* is where you will find these.

Thinking Through My Own Worldview

When I was in my twenties, I went through a profound conversion experience. However, my experience might have been unusual because I worked it out in my head first, and then my heart followed. For many people, it is the reverse.

I had to start by questioning whether or not I believed God was real. I had a sense of his presence in my life, so I have to acknowledge that I was predisposed to accept his existence. In addition to my predisposition, the complexity of creation also spoke to me of an undeniable intelligence and a plan behind life and the fact of our existence. While other arguments also supported my belief in God, these were probably the most influential.

Okay. So God exists, but what about Jesus? What about the Bible? Did it make sense that God revealed himself through Scripture? Coming up with answers that agreed with the basics of Christianity, I realized that I needed to start working on developing a real relationship with God. I quickly came to see that God's purpose for my life had to take priority over my own.

That was only the beginning. I hadn't worked through

all of the important questions I needed to face, and I hadn't thought much about the Catholic Church in particular. I had dealt with worldview questions only far enough to form a broadly Christian belief system. That made it easy for me to start attending Protestant churches, where I fell in love with Scripture.

It was years later, as I continued asking other worldview and theological questions, that I was finally confronted with the question of church authority. I had dived deeply into the Protestant world and had created the Sunday school program for our Protestant church, a new branch of Calvary Chapel. Meanwhile, I was homeschooling my own children, having begun in the early 1980s when many families were still battling to make homeschooling legal in their states. I became a leader within the homeschool world, serving on the board for our state organization. Along the way, I started reviewing curriculum for homeschoolers and formed a fledgling business around publishing those reviews. Thanks to the expertise I had developed with curriculum, I started speaking at homeschool conferences around the country and, eventually, around the world.

Fairly early in our homeschooling journey, I read Francis Schaeffer's book *How Should We Then Live?* This book re-popularized the concept of worldviews in the evangelical Protestant world, and it turned out to be influential in my life, setting me off on a track to learn more about worldviews. I eventually began teaching worldview courses to homeschoolers. Then I started teaching their parents about worldviews as well, both in local classes as well as at homeschool conferences.

Within my own worldview, educational issues have always been closely aligned with faith. If all areas of life have to do with God, then all subjects taught to children should include discussion—or at least recognition—of God. So in the midst of everything else, I was writing and speaking about educational freedom issues, particularly the need for private schools and homeschools to remain free from government control so that they can faithfully pass on religious beliefs to their students. I wrote a book on that topic that broadened my circles in other directions, giving me opportunities to talk with people with all sorts of beliefs regarding religion, faith, philosophy, and politics. That book opened doors to participate in a number of debates, to talk with many legislators, to participate in many talk show interviews, and to speak at education-issues conferences.

My traveling and interaction with so many different types of people led me into many apologetic discussions. I had such strong convictions about what I believed and why those beliefs were true that I thought I was on solid ground. Except that there was one small, nagging question that I hoped no one would ask me: "How do we know that we have the correct list of books that belong in the New Testament?" I know that sounds like a nit-picky question, but it really is important, and it is the question that ultimately brought me back to the Catholic Church.

I was a Protestant at the time I started investigating that question, and Sola Scriptura (Scripture alone as the final authority) was the bottom line for defending my worldview. I eventually figured out that there was no way to defend the validity of the New Testament without acknowledging the authority of the Catholic Church. If the Catholic Church got it wrong when they approved the books of the New Testament in the late fourth century, then they could have gotten it wrong when they developed doctrines about the Trinity and the nature of Jesus. I concluded that either the Catholic Church was and is led by the Holy Spirit and is a trustworthy source for Truth, or else none of what the Catholic Church teaches is defensible. And if the Catholic Church could have erred when they determined which books were in the New Testament, then Protestants have a false foundation in Sola Scriptura because they might have the wrong collection of books.

When I realized this, I had to make a very difficult decision to leave my Protestant world, which included our social circle, my closest friends who were convinced I was wrong, and my business, which was dependent upon connections in the Protestant world.

When I finally made the decision to return to the Catholic Church after being gone for more than twenty years, it was costly and painful. However, I can honestly say that I have never regretted it. Although it took time, God filled all the holes in my life.

Why Worldviews Matter

Through all of this, I was driven by the need for my worldview to be consistent and coherent. Now, I realize that my need for logical coherence might be stronger than what many others experience. However, I think that people frequently suffer cognitive dissonance (inconsistent thoughts) about faith issues. They think they believe one thing that their parents told them, but a teacher or someone else they revere has told them that the opposite is true. If they love and respect both parties, how do they reconcile the conflicting beliefs? I expect that children suffer from this more than adults. They are told to accept many things without questioning them. They are often put in the middle, not knowing who or what is correct but not at all wanting to challenge or question their authority figures.

As we get older, questioning and challenging becomes more acceptable. Unfortunately, too many people who have grown up with cognitive dissonance about faith issues don't bother searching out correct answers. After all, that takes work and risk. Instead, they jettison faith altogether and become "nones"—they claim no spiritual affiliation at all.

It is important to note that the term *none* is really not a fair descriptor for those who do not align with any recognized religion. Most of them might have rejected traditional forms of religion, but they substitute some other form of faith. They might believe in unseen forces as proposed by movies like Star Wars—movies which are actually based on Eastern philosophies. They might believe in Karma without accepting Hinduism or Buddhism, thinking that there is some supernatural balancing scale working behind the scenes. They might believe in themselves as they follow their hearts rather than rational thought. They might believe that it is up to them to create their own reality. We all operate out of fundamental beliefs of one sort or another.

Getting to the Worldview Questions

As I mentioned earlier, many people have not consciously thought about their worldview. They have absorbed it without analyzing it. Of course, there are some people who have given serious thought to their beliefs and their worldviews, but they seem to be rare.

Whatever the case, we should try to understand the foundational beliefs held by those we hope to evangelize. By raising questions about those foundational beliefs, we might be able to get them to reconsider what they think they believe. The best questions to ask are usually "why?" questions. If someone states that they believe something with which you strongly differ, you can respond with the simple question, "Why do you believe that is true?" Their responses will generally give you at least a few more opportunities to ask other "why?" questions. "What?" questions can also be helpful, questions such as "What do you mean by that?" or "What evidence do you have that what you are saying is true?"

If you want to better understand how worldviews play out in terms of life and death issues, you should read the next chapter, "Worldview Comparison."

Keep in mind that a worldview discussion is not a confrontation or an argument. You want to ask questions to find out what the person thinks and believes, then try to get them to explain why they believe those things. This is not the time to push back with strong resistance. It is far more effective if your questions help them consider other ideas without a direct challenge. Worldview conversations done well leave both participants feeling positive toward one another. It should feel like they have gifted each other with a very personal conversation. The person from whom you are trying to elicit the worldview explanations should feel that you really care and want to understand them. Whether or not you agree with them is not important at this point. This type of conversation is so rare that most people appreciate the opportunity to really be heard at a serious level. If the initial conversation goes well, you will be much more likely to have an opportunity to take the conversation deeper at a later date.

I cannot overemphasize the importance of making yourself available for conversations. I don't enjoy chatting on the telephone without a particular purpose. However, I do call people to stay in touch and know enough about what is happening with them so that I can pray for them with specific prayers and then follow up with questions regarding those issues. Many times these are challenging, traumatic, or painful issues that give me natural openings to discuss the important things that are happening in their lives. It also gives me opportunities to bring up faith perspectives in the context of their challenging life issues and to help them explore their own worldviews.

Discussion Questions

1. Have you ever gotten bogged down into a fruitless conversation about spiritual matters because the conversation started with a peripheral question?

2. Before reading this book, had you ever considered the idea of worldview?

3. Have you recognized inconsistencies in your own worldview?

4. Have you ever seriously questioned or examined your own theological beliefs?

5. If you know someone who claims to have no spiritual beliefs, can you figure out what it is that they put in the place of God? For what do they voluntarily sacrifice their time and energy and devotion?

6. If someone were to say to you, "All religions are equally true and all lead to the same place," what sort of questions might you ask to challenge that thinking?

Books such as *The Universe Next Door* by James Sire, *Finding Truth* by Nancy Pearcey, and *Understanding the Times* by Jeff Myers and David A. Noebel explain and contrast numerous worldviews in far more depth than I can do here. Note that all three of these classic works on worldview were written by Protestants, so there are points of disagreement with Catholic teaching. Catholic authors have addressed worldviews in a more limited form in a number of books such as:

- *Catholicism and Reason* by Rev. Edward J. Hayes, Rev. Msgr. Paul J. Hayes, and James J. Drummey (plus four other books in the series)
- *How to Do Apologetics: Making the Case for Our Faith* by Patrick Madrid
- *Orthodoxy* by G. K. Chesterton

- *Thoughtful Theism: Redeeming Reason in an Irrational Age* by Andrew Younan
- *Why I Am Catholic (and You Should Be Too)* by Brandon Vogt
- *Why We're Catholic: Our Reasons for Faith, Hope, and Love* by Trent Horn

CHAPTER 9

WORLDVIEW COMPARISON

Jesus, you are the Way, the Truth, and the Life.
Please lead us into a deeper understanding of
what this means in our lives. Amen.

Understanding worldviews is so important to evangelism that I want to expand upon this more concretely. However, I realize that some of my readers might not yet be interested in exploring worldviews more deeply at this point. If that's the case for you, you can skip this chapter for now.

In this chapter, I want to clarify how worldviews influence a person's values and beliefs about other issues so that you can see why steering a conversation toward worldview questions might be most effective.

While there are many other "religious" options people might choose—various Christian denominations, Judaism, Buddhism, Wicca, Hinduism, Scientology, and others—I am going to compare Christianity with the most common alternative to Christianity in the United States: secular humanism.

First, we need to understand what secular humanism is. The Council for Secular Humanism explains it on their website: "Secular humanism is nonreligious, espousing no belief in a realm or beings imagined to transcend ordinary experience. Secular humanism is a *lifestance*. . . . As a *secular lifestance*, secular humanism incorporates the Enlightenment principle of *individualism*, which celebrates emancipating the individual from traditional controls by family, church, and state, increasingly empowering each of us to set the terms of his or her own life."[K]

Note the emphasis on individualism as well as the rejection of authorities such as family, church, and state. These ideas are extremely powerful (and popular) in our current culture. If we comprehend the underlying beliefs, we can more easily understand why someone might choose not to ever marry, or might choose to have children and think nothing of deserting them, or might object to any sort of moral restrictions that might inhibit his or her own self-fulfillment. This definition of secular humanism makes it clear that God has no place in this worldview.

Just as Catholicism provides the basis for a comprehensive worldview, the same is true with secular humanism. "Secular humanism is comprehensive, touching every aspect of life including issues of values, meaning, and identity. Thus it is broader than atheism, which concerns only the nonexistence of god or the supernatural. Important as that may be, there's a lot more to life . . . and secular humanism addresses it."[L]

Archbishop Charles Chaput contrasts the underlying beliefs of Catholics and secular humanists, saying, "The Christian understanding of human dignity claims that we're made in the image and likeness of God. . . . But this grounding in God is exactly what the modern spirit rejects as an insult to human sovereignty."[M]

From their own description, you can see how secular humanism accurately describes widely-held views in modern American culture. Belief in a God to whom we are accountable is rejected. Instead, under secular humanism, we become our own gods—we are the only ones who get to decide the purpose of our life. We get to establish our own system of morality or choose to follow no moral code at all.

In the chart below, you can see that Christianity and secular humanism offer different answers to the most important worldview questions.

Is There a God?	
Christianity	Secular Humanism
Yes	No

What Is the Nature of Man?	
Christianity	Secular Humanism
Man is a being created by God in his image and likeness.	Man is an accidental product of random evolution. "There is no God and no deity, there is only us, the material world, and the ecosystem surrounding us. There is no soul and super nature, everything, including ourselves, are made of materials."[N]

What Happens When We Die?	
Christianity	Secular Humanism
We continue in existence through eternity either in the presence of God or apart from him.	Nothing. There is no life after death. "Humanists believe that we only live once, that this life is 'not a dress rehearsal.'. . . The idea of a non-material existence after we die doesn't make sense to many humanists."[O]

What Is the Purpose of Life?	
Christianity	Secular Humanism
"Endowed with a spiritual soul, with intellect and with free will, the human person is from his very conception ordered to God and destined for eternal beatitude. He pursues his perfection in 'seeking and loving what is true and good'."[P] Or in the words of the Baltimore Catechism, "God made us to show forth His goodness and to share with us His everlasting happiness in heaven."[Q]	"Humanists affirm that humans have the freedom to give meaning, value, and purpose to their lives by their own independent thought, free inquiry, and responsible, creative activity."[R]

How Do We Know Right From Wrong?	
Christianity	Secular Humanism
Moral truth is objective, meaning that it is not relative to subjective whims of a culture or individuals. God is the ultimate source of all moral truth. We have an innate sense of basic moral truth based upon natural law. Since sin can interfere with our ability to discern correct morality, God has directly revealed moral guidelines in Scripture such as those expressed in the Ten Commandments and the Sermon on the Mount. The Catholic Church also offers specific guidelines.[S]	"Secular humanists hold that ethics is consequential, to be judged by results. This is in contrast to so-called command ethics, in which right and wrong are defined in advance and attributed to divine authority. . . . Secular humanists seek to develop and improve their ethical principles by examining the results they yield in the lives of real men and women."[T]

So What?

What we believe about basic worldview questions colors our thinking about other areas of life. There is no guarantee that any person is going to be entirely consistent in expressing or living out his or her worldview, but there are implications that follow from different belief systems.

I'll demonstrate this by beginning with just one of the

basic questions: "What is the nature of man?" We'll follow this question to just a few of the logical conclusions. As you can see in the chart, each succeeding belief is built upon the previous one, logically following from the belief about who man is. In this case, I'll focus in on Catholic teaching in contrast to that of secular humanists.

What Is the Nature of Man?	
Catholic	Secular Humanist
Man is made in the image and likeness of God.	Man is an accidental product of random evolution.
Each person has an immortal soul created by God.	Human beings have no soul in the sense of a dimension of themselves that is both spiritual and eternal.
Every human life has intrinsic value.	Human life has no intrinsic value other than what any one of us might personally assign to it.
All people are created by God, and only God has the right to determine when someone should die. (Capital punishment adds another dimension to this issue that I'm not going to address here.)	Self-determination is paramount. It should be up to the individual in most cases to make decisions regarding his or her own life. "Because humanists take happiness and suffering as foremost moral considerations, quality of life will often trump the preservation of life at all costs."[U]

Because God is the author of life, we have no right to end the life of the unborn through abortion.	The needs of those already living are more important than a "potential life," so abortion is an acceptable choice. "I am pro-abortion like I'm pro-knee replacement and pro-chemotherapy and pro-cataract surgery. As the last protection against ill-conceived childbearing when all else fails, abortion is part of a set of tools that help women and men to form the families of their choosing. I believe that abortion care is a positive social good."[V]
Life begins at conception. In vitro fertilization generally results in the destruction of surplus fertilized embryos—the destruction of life—so this is morally evil.	In vitro fertilization provides a needed service for those with fertility issues or for those who conceive a child who will be born with genetic problems or deformities. Parents are entitled to seek their own happiness. The destroyed embryos have no value as individual human beings. "Conception is the start of something, but it is more the start of the possible rather than the actual. It is not until a being emerges that has the traits necessary for individual existence that we can and should say that a person has begun"[W]

In summary, secular humanist bioethics do not have reliable moral guidelines based on a moral authority beyond the individual person. Secular humanism has difficulty showing that any medical procedure can be intrinsically wrong unless it is done without the permission of the person undergoing the procedure. Of course, in the case of the unborn or those unable to speak up for themselves, they do not get to express their preference. Try picturing yourself in the place of a person in a long-term coma. Would you prefer to have a doctor with Catholic or secular humanist beliefs guiding his recommendations about your care?

My point is that you can see how attitudes and beliefs are generally based upon underlying assumptions or beliefs. This is why it is usually best to avoid starting a discussion, for example, about whether it is acceptable for a person to take his or her own life. If you do not discuss the underlying beliefs first, you are not going to get to the heart of the issue, and it is unlikely that you will change anyone's mind. For them, it simply boils down to "You have no right to tell me what to think about this." If they don't acknowledge that life comes from God and that we are accountable to him, then their view makes sense.

So if you want a conversation like this to actually progress in a useful direction, it makes sense to try to reroute the conversation to the underlying worldview-based beliefs first. This clearly takes time. You cannot expect to have someone change their mind about their entire worldview based upon one conversation. Generally, this happens through a series of conversations and experiences that spring from situations where a person starts to reconsider what he or she believes and becomes open to the possibility that what they have held to be true might not be so.

If someone close to you has a secular humanist worldview or another non-Catholic worldview, you need to be aware of the "teachable moments" when something in their life happens that might give them cause to rethink fundamental beliefs. At that point, you don't preach at them, but you ask probing worldview questions that help them think it through for themselves.

For example, maybe someone they know has just committed suicide and they are struggling with the loss of that person and conflicted by their claimed belief that their friend's choice to commit suicide was appropriate and acceptable. You might bring up a question, cautiously phrased, such as, "What do you think happens to us when we die?" That question might open the door to consideration of the possibility of an afterlife even if your friend has denied it in the past.

You cannot control these conversations and guide them in a predictable direction. You have to pray and trust the Holy Spirit to be at work, to give you the words you need, and the discernment as to when to talk and when to just listen.

Ethics and Worldviews

We need to realize that when we enter into conversations with those holding other worldviews, especially secular humanism, we are likely to run into huge disagreements over many issues. As Catholics, we have a foundation for moral decision-making based ultimately on the two Great

Commandments: love God above all else and love your neighbor as yourself.

In case that is not concrete enough for us, both the Bible and Catholic teaching provide specifics such as the last of the Ten Commandments, "You shall not covet your neighbor's wife, his male or female slave, his ox or donkey, or anything that belongs to your neighbor," or the prohibition against abortion (or other innocent life) in the *Catechism of the Catholic Church* (2258): "Human life is sacred because from its beginning it involves the creative action of God and it remains forever in a special relationship with the Creator, who is its sole end. God alone is the Lord of life from its beginning until its end: no one can under any circumstance claim for himself the right directly to destroy an innocent human being." A secular humanist, on the other hand, has no outside direction, other than the civil law and the influence of friends and family, as to how to make moral decisions.

You might recall the popular television series *24* that starred Keifer Sutherland as counter-terrorist agent Jack Bauer. Bauer's approach to problem solving seemed to be based upon his own personal needs and preferences, no matter the legality or wisdom of his actions. Lying, disobeying orders, following his own agenda, and torturing prisoners all seemed to be justified since Bauer was the hero of each season's convoluted tale. The *24* series is only one example of what has become increasingly common in television and movies: a conflicted hero who makes moral decisions in the moment based on little more than his own gut feelings.

Clearly, the Jack Bauer character wasn't the first television or movie role exhibiting muddled morality. We can go back a number of decades to the many movies where adults are clueless and the children decide for themselves what to do to save the day. Disney's *Parent Trap* from 1961, *E.T. the Extra-Terrestrial* from 1982, and *Home Alone* from 1990 are classic examples. Millions of people enjoyed watching these movies, but just as in many other movies and television shows, disobedience, lying, stealing, and disrespect for adults are implicitly approved as the children rescue each situation.

This is moral relativism—morality is determined in the moment only in relation to one's present thoughts, needs, and feelings. Moral relativism is a natural result of a secular humanist worldview.

When it comes to morality, if there is no authority outside of man to whom we are accountable, that leaves each person as his own judge. Of course, the government has power to enforce some forms of morality, but these enforcements too often seem arbitrary and inconsistent. The rampant moral relativism in our culture is why younger generations tend to believe that they can do whatever they want "as long as it doesn't hurt anyone else."

This should provoke serious concern. In my experience, when I comment upon morality portrayed in the media, I tend to get responses like, "It's just a movie. Lighten up." Unfortunately, television and movies have been a much stronger influence in the lives of most of those under the age of seventy-five than have any sources of positive ethics such as faith and family. The subtle influence, repeated time after time, has had a very real effect in introducing moral relativism into our culture to the extent that even those who claim to be Christians sometimes operate as moral relativists.

Most people consider themselves ethical, but few can tell you the basis for their ethics. Robert Kraynak writes about the resulting dilemmas our modern culture experiences in regard to ethics, a dilemma resulting from relativistic attitudes. Kraynak observes:

> What is so strange about our age is that demands for respecting human rights and human dignity are *increasing* even as the foundations for those demands are disappearing. In particular, beliefs in man as a creature made in the image of God, or an animal with a rational soul are being replaced by a scientific materialism that undermines what is noble and special about man, and by doctrines of relativism that deny the objective morality required to undergird human dignity. How do we account for the widening gap between metaphysics and morals today? How do we explain "justice without foundations" — a virtue that seems to exist like a table without legs, suspended in mid-air? What is holding up the central moral beliefs of our times?[X]

Moral relativism is yet another reason to avoid conversations that focus first on the peripheral issues that have a moral dimension—issues such as living together without marriage, the death penalty, abortion, and same-sex marriage—and instead try to discuss more fundamental worldview issues such as the existence of God and the purpose of life. Changing a person's moral compass from one based on relativism rather than absolute values is foundational, but it is unlikely to happen unless a person accepts the existence of God and man's moral accountability to him.

The Problem of Scientism

Scientism is one of the common beliefs that has increasingly taken hold of those operating from a secular humanist worldview. As Bishop Robert Barron writes, scientism is "the philosophical assumption that the real is reducible to what the empirical sciences can verify or describe. . . . That there might be a dimension of reality knowable in a non-scientific but still rational manner never occurs to them." Barron goes on to argue that scientism prejudices its adherents against things we might know from religion as well as from literature, philosophy, metaphysics, and mysticism. The dependence upon science has become so strong that many people dismiss as superstition, fantasy, or primitive belief anything that cannot be explained by science.[Y]

This attitude has been reinforced by the educational system and the media to the point where bringing up God as an explanatory cause or influence is ridiculed. If God is taken out of the picture, science is substituted as the explanatory force behind everything, including the existence of the universe, the existence of man, consciousness, love, creativity, and beauty.

Scientism poses such a formidable barrier to faith that it often must be addressed before you can make any spiritual headway in a conversation. Someone who holds to scientism almost certainly believes that God and science stand in opposition to one another, so that issue should usually be addressed first. It might be fairly easy to do so if the person with whom you are speaking is willing to consider historical facts. As Bishop Barron points out,

> The vast majority of the founding figures of modern science—Copernicus, Newton, Kepler, Descartes, Pascal, Tycho Brahe—were devoutly religious. More to it, two of the most important physicists of the 19th century—Faraday and Maxwell—were extremely pious, and the formulator of the Big Bang theory was a priest! If you want a contemporary embodiment of the coming-together of science and religion, look to John Polkinghorne, Cambridge particle physicist and Anglican priest and one of the best commentators on the non-competitive interface between scientific and religious paths to truth. Indeed, as Polkinghorne and many others have pointed out, the modern physical sciences were, in fact, made possible by the religious milieu out of which they emerged.[z]

That religious milieu included a deeply Christian culture that dominated the Western world for centuries before and after the era when modern science began to emerge.

Bishop Barron goes on to summarize two key reasons why Christianity served to even make science possible. Christianity claims that the universe is created. It is not divine, and it has no capricious mind of its own. It is part of creation. Secondly, the world is intelligible, reflecting a creative intelligence behind its design. It is only because it is intelligible that scientists can have confidence that they will come up with rational explanations and results from their observations and experiments. If it were not intelligible, scientists could have no confidence in their findings (i.e., that they could be predictable and consistent). Even findings such as Newton's theory of gravity would not have been considered reliable, and they would not have been able to extrapolate from data to come up with continuing advances and developments of those theories.

Once someone accepts the reality that science and Christianity are not in conflict with one another, you are still not out of the woods. You might also have to address evolution and creation, since the predominant materialistic evolutionary view (as opposed to a theistic evolutionary view) leaves no room for God.

You might be able to address the concept of God as creator without necessarily having to get into evolution. Thomas Aquinas's five arguments for the existence of God have stood the test of time fairly well. The arguments follow five different lines of reasoning:

- The argument from motion
- The argument from causation
- The argument from contingency
- The argument from degree
- The argument from design

I appreciate Theodore Gracyk's easy-to follow summary of each argument that he presents in an article titled "Thomas Aquinas: The Existence of God can be proven in five ways."[AA]

Modern science increasingly points to an intelligent designer. For example, the amazing complexity of even a single living cell defies all mathematical odds of accidentally coming into existence, even gradually over billions of years. Books such as Stephen Meyer's *Signature in the Cell* and Michael Behe's *Darwin's Black Box* provide solid, cutting-edge scientific evidence for an intelligence behind the creation of living things. Catholics would do well to read up on the scientific evidence that buttresses their faith rather than avoid conversations about this hugely important topic.

Discussion Questions

1. What evidence of secular humanist worldviews have you observed in either your immediate culture or in the broader American culture?

2. Have you ever been involved in a conversation about abortion or a similar issue where you felt like you were just talking past one another because of drastically different underlying worldviews? Do you think shifting to worldview questions might have helped? Why or why not?

3. What examples of moral relativism have you noticed in television or movies? Were you aware of it at the time or is this a new insight?

4. How might you answer someone's claim that they should be able to do whatever they want if it doesn't hurt anyone else?

5. Have you come up against scientism in a personal conversation? How did you handle it?

CHAPTER 10

WORLDVIEW QUESTIONS FOR PROTESTANTS

*Lord Jesus, help us to yearn for the unity of your Church just
as you told your disciples that we might be one in you so that
the world will know that you were sent by the Father. Amen.*

Many Catholics are concerned about bringing their
family members, relatives, and friends back into the
Church. While some leave the Catholic Church without
forming any other religious affiliations, many are attracted
to Protestantism. The U.S. Religious Landscape Survey by
the Pew Research Center's Forum on Religion & Public Life
reported, "Almost half of those leaving the Church become
unaffiliated and almost half become Protestant."[AB]

While a top priority for many of us is the return of those
who were formerly Catholic, we should also want to bring
our separated Christian brothers and sisters who were never
Catholic into the fullness of faith found only in the Catholic
Church.

However, Protestants who prefer being part of churches

that place few demands upon them might not be interested in becoming Catholic. As Protestant churches have contended with challenges from the surrounding culture, some have lightened up their moral and doctrinal standards to maintain membership rolls. The Catholic Church often stands alone or with few allies on the cultural battlefield as she continues to insist on a traditional view of marriage and sex only within marriage. The Church also finds herself with little support as she holds the line against birth control, abortion, in vitro fertilization, and euthanasia. Those looking for a "comfortable" church are not likely to find it in Catholicism.

On the other hand, as I discussed in chapter 2, those Protestants most inclined to join the Catholic Church are those familiar with Scripture and church history. These people are willing to make an honest assessment of the claims the Catholic Church makes.

The worldview issues I've addressed thus far might be your starting point with some of those you hope to evangelize, but biblically literate Protestants have entirely different worldview issues. Protestants generally have a Christian worldview but not a Catholic worldview. While both Protestants and Catholics might have similar answers to questions about the existence of God, the person of Jesus, the nature of man, and even about most moral issues, there are some critical differences in the makeup of their worldviews. There are five key areas of difference:

- Church authority, including the hierarchy, infallibility, and the teaching magisterium

- The communion of saints and prayer to saints
- The role of Mary
- Sacraments
- Purgatory

That means the worldview questions you might discuss with them could be one or two levels beyond those you would discuss with a non-Christian. Nevertheless, there are still some questions that are foundational to others.

For example, a common Protestant attack against Catholicism is that Catholics worship Mary. You could respond by trying to defend the *veneration* of Mary (meaning to honor or hold in high esteem) in contrast to worship. But a more foundational issue to discuss is the communion of saints. You might ask, "What happens to Christians when they die? Do they stop being members of the Body of Christ? Are they aware of what is happening on Earth?" You could to Hebrews 12:1, a verse that describes the great cloud of witnesses, those saints who have gone before us and who seem to be very aware of what is happening on Earth. If a Protestant begins to think of the Body of Christ as including those who have gone before us to be with God, and they understand that they are aware in some way of what happens on Earth, then they can begin to grasp the concept of praying to the saints for intercession. It might also help to point out that they routinely ask for the prayers of friends and family, not because they think others can answer that prayer, but because they can pray to God on their behalf; it is no different with the saints, or Mary, for that matter. Catholic teaching about

Mary becomes more understandable with this in mind since she is the most important intercessor of all.

Protestants also require biblical texts to support theological positions. However, their reliance on Sola Scriptura is predicated on their certainty that they have a Bible that is absolutely reliable. You can ask questions such as, "Which came first: the Church or the Bible?" (The Church came first and created the Bible.) This might lead into a discussion about the compilation of the Bible, particularly the New Testament. It is clear from church history that the Church determined which books would make up the New Testament. That makes the Bible reliant upon the Church. Other questions stem from that: "Did the Holy Spirit guide the Church as it decided which books would comprise the New Testament or might the Church have been in error?" Church authority is the real issue here. It is a critical point because if the Church erred in the early centuries as it worked out doctrines of the Trinity and the nature of Jesus along with the content of the Bible, then no Christian denomination has a leg on which to stand. On the other hand, if the Church was led by the Holy Spirit and we can trust in Jesus's promise that he would send the Holy Spirit to guide his Church, then the discussion might be about whether or not the Catholic Church continues to have that same guidance or not. This sort of discussion can cause a Protestant to reevaluate his or her belief in Sola Scriptura, a doctrinal position that is foundational for most Protestants. When all else fails, ask them to tell you where it says in the Bible that the Bible is the only source of authority. (Hint: it doesn't!)

I do not have space to delve into these key topics in

depth here. There are many other resources that can help prepare you for conversations with Protestants. Some of the most useful are the books of conversion stories by Protestant leaders who converted to Catholicism. They all have had to wrestle with these basic questions, although one or another of those questions might have been more important in each of their journeys. In addition to some of the books and resources I have listed in chapter 4, you might want to check out *The Case for Catholicism* by Trent Horn and stories of Catholic "Reverts" (those who left the Catholic Church but then returned) at the *Why I'm Catholic* website.[5]

While you might find that Protestants who are well-versed in their faith are willing to enter into a worldview or theological conversation, this might not be the case with former Catholics. Thomas Reese's article "The hidden exodus: Catholics becoming Protestants" tells us: "The data shows that disagreement over specific doctrines is not the main reason Catholics become Protestants. We also have lots of survey data showing that many Catholics who stay disagree with specific church teachings. Despite what theologians and bishops think, doctrine is not all that important either to those who become Protestant or to those who stay Catholic." Reese also points out that, based on the Pew Research Center's U.S. Religious Landscape Survey, they discovered that "people are not becoming Protestants because they disagree with specific Catholic teachings; people are leaving

---

5   "Catholic Reverts," *Why I'm Catholic,* www.whyimcatholic.com/index.php/conversion-stories/catholic-reverts.

because the Church does not meet their spiritual needs and they find Protestant worship service better."[AC]

So the Pew study tells us that theological arguments and worldview questions might be of little use with many Catholics who have left the Faith. They are more concerned with their personal experience than with doctrinal accuracy. However, many Protestants, including former Catholics, become serious about their faith and continue to learn and grow through Bible study, worship, prayer, and fellowship with other Christians. Over time, they might reach a point where they dig deep enough to encounter the truth about the Catholic Church, but there are barriers that discourage them from pursuing any investigation in that direction.

Protestants are often tied to their church by a tight network of relationships. Their friends all attend church with them, and their social life revolves around these friends as well as church activities. Their children also have their own friendships and activities through the church. Protestants tend to be much more strongly connected socially to their churches than Catholics. That presents us with an entirely different problem. These people will have to recreate many of their personal and social relationships if they become Catholic, a daunting and off-putting challenge.

If for some reason those social connections within their Protestant world break down, it presents a point of vulnerability where a Protestant might be open to considering the Catholic Church. This is often precipitated by something like a church split or a scandal with the pastor. Protestant churches split over seemingly minor issues such as the style of worship music or the pastor's leadership style, but they also split over major issues such as the ordination of women or the church's position on same-sex marriage. Whatever the impetus, these disruptions cause Protestant churches to divide into camps, and the results are rarely edifying. Division within a church sometimes causes Protestants to think more deeply about church structure and governance as well as doctrinal issues. This is a time when you might be able to have a discussion about important issues such as church authority and the consistency of church doctrine, raising questions that are often unanswerable from a Protestant perspective.

Having those theological discussions is important, but remember that Protestants might well be risking social alienation on a large scale. Is your parish a warm and welcoming place where they can easily build new social relationships? Sadly, that's rarely true of Catholic parishes. Many parishes are so large that people can come to Mass week after week without encountering anyone who can greet them by name. It generally takes extra effort to get to meet people and form relationships within Catholic parishes. Keep this in mind if you are inviting a Protestant to consider the Catholic Church. You might have to personally endeavor to make introductions and connections for this person.

Does Your Parish Preach the Gospel?

Many Protestants are convinced that the Catholic Church does not teach the importance of having a personal relationship with Jesus Christ. We have to acknowledge that the Catholic Church has not always stressed this point. To an objective observer, it might have looked like the Church was more focused on processing people through sacramental preparation classes than on ensuring that they have a relationship with Jesus. That certainly remains true in some parishes today.

However, Pope St. John Paul II, Pope Benedict XVI, and Pope Francis have all understood and promoted the proclamation of the basic kerygma, the Gospel message that Jesus died for us and wants to offer to us the free gift of salvation. While the centrality of the kerygma is much more widely recognized in the Catholic Church today than twenty or thirty years ago, the importance of the kerygma trickles slowly and unevenly down to the parish level.

A reordering of priorities to put that relationship with Jesus front and center has definitely accelerated in recent years. I see and hear about it happening at Catholic parishes around the country and abroad. I experience it personally within our parish where we have been running the Alpha program for three years and working on other evangelistic efforts before that.

However, I know that this is not the situation in every parish. If we hope to attract Protestants to the Catholic Church, we have to be aware of the spiritual health and evangelistic outlook of our parish and maybe of our neighboring parishes. Would a Protestant clearly hear the proclamation of the kerygma at Mass? For example, when the day's Gospel reading deals directly with salvation, does the homilist use that opportunity to remind us of the importance of repentance and being in relationship with God? Or are the homilies geared more toward the social gospel or psychological approaches to spiritual wholeness?

Protestants need reassurance that the Catholic Church does, indeed, proclaim the Gospel. If we want to invite someone to come visit a Catholic parish for Mass or other event, we need to be aware of what the experience is like from his or her point of view. If your parish is weak in this area, you might need to scout out a neighboring parish to identify one that clearly proclaims the basic message of the Gospel so that the Protestant you are trying to draw into the Catholic faith is not merely confirmed in his or her prejudices against Catholicism.

Discussion Questions

1. Have you ever attended a Protestant service? How did social aspects of the experience compare with the experiences within your Catholic parish?

2. Have you ever been challenged with questions from a Protestant? How did you handle the situation?

3. Think about or discuss how you might answer someone who claims that Catholics worship Mary, or that there is no need to be Catholic if one believes that Jesus is his or her Savior.

4. How would you reply if someone said Jesus already paid the price for our salvation and there is nothing we can do to add to that (in other words, claiming that the Catholic Church wrongly says that we earn our salvation by good works)?

CHAPTER 11

LISTENING

*Accepting our weakness and frailty, Lord Jesus, help us
become better listeners, attuned to others so that we can
be conduits of your love and care in their lives. Amen*

As you have read through previous chapters, you might
have gotten a sense that you need to know a lot before
you can start evangelizing. However, while an understanding of doctrine and worldviews is helpful, more often than
not, the most valuable skill you bring to the table for an
evangelistic conversation is the ability to listen.

I think we've all been in situations when we're talking
with someone and we come to the realization they are not
listening. They might be hearing, but they are not really listening—and we all know the difference. I suspect that we've
all been guilty of not really listening ourselves in at least a
conversation or two.

I believe listening is an art, a skill that we can develop,
but we have to intentionally work at it. In some ways, that
can be more challenging than adding to our mental library

of theological knowledge because it requires self-control and sacrifice. Too many of us prefer to be listened to rather than to listen to others.

In this chapter, I want to address the "art of listening," but I want to begin with a story from a very helpful book: *Listen In* by Rachael Crabb, Sonya Reeder, and Diana Calvin. This is a true story told by Rachael Crabb. She now works in church ministry and spends a lot of time helping other people. In the book, she shares a very troubling story from her childhood that had shaped her life up to that time.

When Rachael was a preschooler, her mom went to the hospital to deliver her new baby brother. Tragically, a staph infection ran through that part of the hospital. Seventeen babies died. Rachael's mom and baby brother did not die, but they had to stay a few weeks in the hospital.

You can imagine how much young Rachael, still a preschooler, would have missed her mom. Rachael was so excited when she was told that her mom was coming home. She just couldn't wait.

When they finally came home, it was in an ambulance, and mom and baby were carried in on a stretcher. Rachael described how she was waiting for their arrival, sitting on the edge of the kitchen table between her two older sisters. When they brought her mother in, Rachael began to shout with excitement. Immediately, her older sisters clamped their hands over her mouth. "Shhh! The baby is sleeping."

No one seemed to be aware of Rachel's need to reunite with her mother. Everyone seemed concerned with their sick baby brother and the need to keep the house quiet.

Rachael said that at that point, "she lost her voice." She

had been an outgoing, talkative child, but she learned that what she thought and felt—her needs—were not important. No one was interested in listening to her. So she learned to bury her feelings and her needs deep inside.

Later in Rachael's story, she chronicles being molested by a neighbor from the time she was eight until she was twelve. She never told anyone because she felt that she couldn't, that nobody would want to hear about her problem.

No one knew this side of Rachael because she covered it up with her outgoing personality. She has a "life of the party" type of personality. People felt like they knew her, but she kept her real feelings and thoughts hidden. Rachael didn't start to recover her ability to speak about what was really going on inside her until many years later, and she's still working on it.

There are a lot of people like Rachael, people who are unable to speak up for themselves or who are afraid to talk about what they really think or what is going on deep inside. And there is a flip side to the Rachaels of the world that compounds the problem—the rarity of people who make themselves present to others as listeners. Many people lack listening skills for want of practice, and many people simply do not care to sacrifice the time. The end result is that few people know how to actively listen or how to encourage those like Rachael to find their voices.

There's a selfishness bred by our modern culture that promotes self-absorption. Sadly, some of us are not interested in hearing what other people have to say unless it involves us. And even for those of us who are not so self-absorbed, we probably experience few incentives to develop better listening skills. Mostly, we just don't think about it.

I realize some of us have people we would rather not listen to because of a personality clash or because of some history. However, most of us are prone to pre-judging people we don't know well, thinking things like, "That person isn't interesting," or, "I don't have anything in common with her." We cut off the possibility of conversation with them based on judgments we have made in advance. But even with people with whom we are comfortable and familiar, I think we too often do a poor job of listening.

If you're reading this book, I think it's safe to assume that you care about other people and want what is best for them—that you want to love others as Jesus commands in John 15:12: "This is my commandment, that you love one another as I have loved you."

Most people recognize that if we really care about someone, we should want to listen to them. And, conversely, if we don't care about someone, we convey that message by not listening to them. The challenge for us is to improve our listening skills, both with those we know and with those we might not normally gravitate towards.

Roadblocks to Listening

We can develop our listening skills by working on roadblocks as well as active skills. First, I will address three roadblocks to listening.

The first roadblock is inattentive listening. Too often, we are not fully attentive when someone is speaking to us. Can you imagine Rachael trying to share her story for the first time as an adult, but then finding that the person she's trying to share it with is more interested in the text coming in on her phone? Can you picture how painful that would be?

Even the best of us fail at listening from time to time. We are easily distracted. We might have an upcoming appointment or a particular worry on our mind that keeps us from focusing on what a person is saying.

And let's face it. Some people are really hard to listen to. They go on and on about things that we don't care about. However, we have to consider that God might be calling us to be patient with those people. Their need to talk excessively might mask a much deeper need that they have. I have known people like this, and I have found that after I have listened a great deal, they begin to trust me. Then they open up about more important issues. But it can take a number of boring, one-sided conversations before we reach that point. These situations can be the most difficult. It is hard to control our body language, to resist the urge to fidget or look around when we want out of a conversation.

Sometimes in a conversation we fail to listen attentively because we are busy thinking about what we want to say rather than listening to what the other person is saying. I don't know if this is a selfish thing or if we just want to feel like we're participating in the conversation. Whatever the cause, I think most of us have probably been in a situation where we are trying to formulate what we want to say while someone else is still talking. Maybe we want to be prepared when it's our turn to talk, which is not a selfish or unreasonable thing, but it still is a distraction to listening. No matter our excuse, we are not really hearing them because of it.

There are certainly other distractions that keep us from actively listening, but no matter the distractions, I think most of can do a better job of listening by being fully attentive to others with our body language as well as our ears.

A second roadblock to listening is inappropriate empathy. For me, the classic example of this happens at baby showers, especially baby showers attended only by women. At a baby shower we are supposed to be celebrating the impending birth of a new baby, and it's usually the first baby for the expectant mother. However, too often the guests start talking about their own experiences with childbirth, and it turns into a "one-upmanship" of horror stories—just exactly what an expectant mother doesn't need to hear!

We do this in lots of other settings. Someone is sick and we have to tell them about when we had the same type of illness. Or someone has just accomplished something, but we have to tell about our own accomplishments.

I don't even think we realize how much we do this. We have a natural tendency to relate our own experiences to those of someone else. Sometimes, sharing what we have in common can become the foundation for a deep friendship and is appropriate. But that tendency can just as easily work against a developing friendship. We tend to think that by jumping in with our own story we are showing empathy, but, instead, we are derailing the person's story. We might be preventing him or her from getting to the point of the story.

We also might be trivializing what they are saying when

we jump in with, "I had an experience just like that." Maybe someone is trying to share something that is vitally important to them. Perhaps a woman has just received some devastating news, and her own story gets hijacked by others chiming in with their own experiences. This happens frequently in small groups. The original woman's story gets lost in the chatter. She was motivated to share because she needs support, but, instead, she sets everyone else off onto their own reminiscing.

Too often, we all want to be heard and no one is interested in listening. But there are times in everyone's life when they need someone to just listen to them.

Here is where we really have to listen to the Holy Spirit. If we truly want what is best for others and we are not putting our own priorities first, it is easier to sense the guidance of the Holy Spirit. It sometimes means foregoing the opportunity to tell about one of our own experiences, even if it's a really good story.

A third roadblock to listening is trying to fix the problem. You know what I mean by this. Someone is sharing a problem and the listener starts coming up with solutions. We can be so full of good advice. Psychologists say that men are much more prone to try to fix situations rather than just listen, but I think we women do our fair share of it too. I know I do!

Generally, when someone is sharing their situation or problem with you, they do not want you to fix it (at least not at first). It is safe to assume that unless they ask you directly—"What do you think I should do?"—you shouldn't try to offer a solution. We rarely have enough information about these situations anyway. We might think the solution is obvious, but it almost always is much more complex a situation than we realize. It is generally best to just be quiet and listen rather than offer advice, and that's usually all that people are looking for. Perhaps after some time has gone by and you feel they have been able to vent, you can delicately offer some advice. But all too often that advice comes much too soon, even to the point that we are interrupting them and not even hearing the whole story.

I have talked about three very common roadblocks to good listening. There are certainly others I could discuss, but my goal is to raise awareness rather than cover all of the possibilities.

Becoming Better Listeners

Most of us need to work on the art of listening. We can train ourselves to listen to other people, but one of the best places to begin is by first training ourselves to listen to God.

We talk about prayer as communication with God, but if we do all of the talking, it's a one-way conversation and God can't get a word in. So we can begin by listening to God, being quiet in his presence so that we can really hear what he is saying to us.

We can also become better listeners by getting rid of some of the white noise in our lives. You know what white noise is—the background sounds that we become so accustomed to that we no longer hear them. I was at Mass one Sunday and I heard this strange noise that turned out to be one of those white noise machines that moms use with their babies.

The mother had brought along a white noise machine to help her baby sleep quietly through Mass. It seemed to work, but it was a distraction for others. I understand why a mom would want to keep her baby sleeping through Mass, but the idea struck me as very ironic. Maybe it kept the baby asleep so he would not be a distraction during Mass, but the white noise itself was a guaranteed distraction for everyone else.

This incident got me thinking: how much white noise do we allow or put into our lives that drowns out what we really need to hear from God or from others? White noise can be actual noise such as the television, radio, your music playlist, YouTube videos, or phone calls. But it might be other ways that we busy ourselves with time-eating activities that negate our ability to do other, better things, including making ourselves available to others.

You might be at a stage where you are ready to start practicing active listening, purposely aspiring to improve your skills. Opportunities abound if we just notice them.

I've done a bit of traveling on airplanes for business trips over the years, trips that I take by myself. Over the last few years, I've learned to consciously pray in advance of each flight for God to put me next to someone who needs to tell his or her story. It doesn't happen on every flight, but you can't believe how often people will open up to a stranger on an airplane if you are a good listener. I've had some amazing conversations with people about serious life issues they're going through, and those conversations often end up with a discussion about where they are spiritually. I don't have to say much of anything, just ask questions and listen with my full attention.

You can have those conversations anywhere if you make yourself available. So try to make opportunities for that to happen. For example, don't plan a get-together with someone with your own agenda in mind. Plan to be there to listen to what the other person has to say. It's amazing what comes out when you mentally approach a conversation with that attitude—that you just want to know what's really going on in his or her life. Or if you are going to an event, rather than sticking just with people you already know, ask God to give you an opportunity for a conversation with someone new.

While we need to work at learning how to listen to other people, remember that if we first learn to listen to God, then we are much more likely to view other people through God's eyes, to really care for them and be willing to listen.

Love Drives Evangelism

"But a part of every human love is that its only truly great and enriching if I am ready to deny myself for this other person, to come out of myself, to give of myself. And that is certainly true of our relationship with God, out of which, in the end, all our other relationships grow.

"I must begin by no longer looking at *myself*, but by asking what *he* wants. I must begin by learning to love. That consists precisely in turning my gaze away from myself and toward him. With this attitude I no longer ask, What am I getting for myself, but I simply let myself be guided by him, truly lose myself in Christ; when I abandon myself, let go of myself, then I see,

yes, life is right at last, because otherwise I am far too
narrow for myself. When, so to speak, I go outside,
then it truly begins, then life attains its greatness."

—*Pope Benedict XVI*[AD]

Discussion Questions

1. What "white noise" keeps you from listening to God
   and others or from spending your time more purposely?

2. Have you had an experience where someone really listened to you when you needed it, or have you had difficulty finding someone who would listen well?

3. Have you ever been the listener when someone desper-
   ately needed to be heard?

4. How has listening played a role in your evangelism
   efforts?

CHAPTER 12

PRAYING FOR AND WITH OTHERS

Heavenly Father, we ask that you fill us with your Holy Spirit so that we can feel with your heart the needs of others. Amen.

I've mentioned praying for and with people a number of times already, but this is such a crucial part of evangelism that I want to offer more specific ideas about how to do this. I'll first talk about praying for others when they are not present, and then I'll discuss ways to pray with people who are with you.

Praying at a Distance

"I'm so sorry to hear that you've lost your job. I'll be praying for you."

How often do we say things like this and then never follow through with prayer? It's not that we should never say this, but if we do, we need to really mean it. After all, offering to pray for someone is not the same as saying, "Have a nice day," or it shouldn't be.

I've found that a great way to follow through on this type of prayer commitment is to keep a prayer journal. I've had nicely bound journals, and I've used spiral notebooks. It doesn't matter what you use so long as you find one central place to record these prayer requests.

When I enter a prayer request in my journal, I keep the entry brief—just enough so that I can pray specifically rather than just naming the person for whom I am praying. For example, if someone has cancer, I will note that down.

I will check periodically to see how things are going. You don't want to be a bother to the person for whom you are praying by checking in too frequently. Unless you are praying about something like a job interview happening next week or another event happening in the near future, you will generally be praying on an ongoing basis for a month or more. Some prayers might be in your journal for years or for the unforeseen future. Of course, God can supply a miraculous cure or a surprising answer to prayer right away, but often we won't be expecting a significant change in status for at least a few months. For this reason, I date my prayer requests. I add a note to the request if something changes and the prayer request needs to change.

In most cases, I will add a date indicating that the prayer was answered or how the situation developed. I have occasionally let a prayer request lapse when I lost touch with the situation and wasn't likely to reconnect in the future. However, most of the time I will keep a prayer request open for years if need be.

There have been a number of long-term prayer requests that have been eventually answered in amazing ways, so I don't give up. Think of the story in chapter 18 of the Gospel of Luke (1–8) where the persistent widow kept pleading with the judge until he responded. Jesus told this parable to encourage his listeners to be persistent in prayer like the widow. Jesus drove home the point saying, "Will not God then secure the rights of his chosen ones who call out to him day and night? Will he be slow to answer them? I tell you, he will see to it that justice is done for them speedily."

If you try to get too elaborate or complicated with your prayer journal, you are not likely to continue with it. So keep it simple. An entry might look like this:

- Shyla Jones – husband asked for divorce 3/12/17

This type of request is going to have an answer one way or the other. They will reconcile or they will divorce. So I will note what happens and a date. Even if they reconcile or divorce, the situation will likely require continued prayer. I might add a note regarding the additional prayer needed, or I might create a new entry. I put a light line through resolved prayer requests. I don't want them to become unreadable because I need to be able to recall how God answered these prayers.

I go through my prayer journal almost every day during my prayer time. I repeat the prayer petitions that remain open, and I thank God for some of the most recent responses since they will be in between the continuing petitions. Periodically, I go back further through my prayer journal and thank God for how he has answered so many of the prayers. It's so easy to forget how faithfully God answers prayers without reminders such as this.

You might want to buttress your prayers by asking for the intercession of Our Blessed Mother or particular saints as you pray through the petitions. You might pray the Memorare or the Hail Mary in particular. I always conclude my prayer time with the Our Father. There is no one correct way to do this, but I have found that developing a routine and a regular time for this type of prayer ensures that it happens rather being relegated to "whenever I get to it."

Praying With Others in Person

If someone tells me about a problem and asks for prayer, they are sometimes surprised if I say, "Could I pray with you about this right now?" Many people have never experienced spontaneous prayer of this sort, and they might be uncomfortable at the prospect. It is possible that someone might put you off saying, "Not right now," or something like that. Still, most of the time, they will let you pray. If you can phrase your offer to pray in such a way that they know you don't expect them to say the prayer, it often helps remove any anxiety they might have.

I find that holding hands while praying with others seems the most comfortable for most situations. Occasionally, I will put my hand on someone's shoulder or back. It depends upon the situation whether or not touching them is appropriate. You can picture many different types of situations where it would vary. A woman praying for a man, or vice versa, might be more appropriately done without touching; just fold your hands and bow your head. If you are praying for a friend, you would very likely be holding hands or touching them. If you're uncertain, you can always ask: "Could we hold hands while we pray?" Or, "Would you mind if I put my hand on your shoulder while I pray?"

These types of prayer experiences can be amazing, no matter the outcome of the actual prayer. People know that you take prayer seriously, that you believe that God is listening to our prayers, and that there is hope in prayer.

You might pray like this with someone who doesn't even know whether or not they believe in God. If that prayer is answered, you can be sure that they will be thinking more deeply about the reality of God. I can't think of a better way to introduce a person to God than through a shared prayer experience!

Follow Up

If I have prayed with someone in person, I will usually also enter that prayer request in my prayer journal. As with other petitions in my journal, I will try to follow up to see how God is answering that prayer.

As I pray through prayer requests in my journal, I bring these people to mind. It makes it easier to love others when you get involved in their lives in this way. My own concerns seem petty compared to those of the people for whom I am praying. I have found that praying for and with others is a very practical way to "die to myself."

Discussion Questions

1. Do you find it awkward or uncomfortable to pray spontaneously with others?

2. Do you have a structured prayer routine that you follow every day? If not, what might work for you?

3. What do you think of the idea of keeping a prayer journal?

4. Have you had opportunities to practice praying in person with others? What opportunities can you envision in your life where you could do this?

5. If you are discussing this with a group, this would be a perfect time to practice praying together for one another's needs.

CHAPTER 13

SUMMARY

By now, I hope you realize that you do not need formal training in apologetics before you can enter into discussions about faith issues. Evangelizing might be as simple as sharing your own stories about what God has done in your life. However, listening to others and praying with and for them should generally be your two top strategies. These strategies are premised on the idea that you are asking good questions to lead the conversation in fruitful directions. Good questions often serve the purpose of revealing the foundational worldview beliefs of the other person since understanding his or her worldview might be essential before you can converse about faith-related topics or cultural issues.

Learning to ask good question does take some practice, but the more you study and know your faith, the easier it is to come up with good questions, as well as good answers to their questions. While I have downplayed the role of apologetics in this book, I have to acknowledge that study is often critical for developing credibility. We need to be able to answer some of the basic questions with confidence and clarity, or our ignorance of our faith might make everything we say less credible.

I want to close with some basic principles to keep in mind when participating in evangelism.

1. Pray about evangelism. Ask God to give you opportunities and to assist you in those conversations.

2. Stay calm and friendly. Getting into arguments never convinces people to change their minds.

3. Remember that love for others is our motivation. If someone doesn't feel loved at the end of the conversation, then you will have failed.

4. Tell your own stories when appropriate, but try to listen more than you talk.

5. If you don't know how to address a question, admit it, go learn about it, and plan a follow-up conversation if possible. This is better than guessing at an answer that might be wrong, and often people will respect your humility in admitting there is something you don't know.

6. Be compassionate. Be willing to hear criticism of the Church without reacting defensively if that is an important part of someone's story or concern.

7. It's not about you. Conversion is the work of the Holy Spirit. We are given the opportunity to share in that work, but only through God's grace.

NOTES

A   Matthew Bunson, "Convocation of Catholic Leaders: 'More Than a Physical Location,'" *National Catholic Register*, July 4, 2017, Accessed November 20, 2017, www.ncregister.com/daily-news/more-than-a-physical-location.

B   Charles J. Chaput, *Strangers in a Strange Land: Living the Christian Faith in a Post-Christian World* (New York: Henry Holt, 2017), p. 190.

C   "September 1, 2017 - A conversation with Michael Cromartie," interview, *Listening In* (podcast), accessed November 18, 2017, world.wng.org/podcast/listening in on September 1, 2017.

D   William Lane Craig, "The Absurdity of Life without God," *Reasonable Faith,* accessed January 30, 2018, www.reasonablefaith.org/writings/popular-writings/existence-nature-of-god/the-absurdity-of-life-without-god/.

E   Benjamin Wormald, "Religious Landscape Study: Beliefs and Practices," *Pew Research Center's Religion & Public Life Project*, May 11, 2015, accessed September 1, 2017, www.pewforum.org/religious-landscape-study/belief-in-god/#beliefs-and-practices; Benjamin Wormald, "Religious Landscape Study: Social and Political Views," *Pew Research Center's Religion & Public Life Project*, May 11, 2015, accessed September 1,

2017, www.pewforum.org/religious-landscape-study/belief-in-god/#social-and-political-views.

F   Don Everts, and Doug Schaupp, *I Once Was Lost: What Postmodern Skeptics Taught Us about Their Path to Jesus* (Downers Grove, IL: IVP Books, 2008).

G   Billy Graham Evangelistic Association, "Begin Your Journey to Peace," *PeacewithGod.net*, accessed April 13, 2018, peacewithgod.net/.

H   Clive Staples Lewis, "Is Theology Poetry?" Essay originally presented in 1944 at an Oxford debating society called the "Socratic Club," accessed November 2, 2017, augustinecollective.org/wp-content/uploads/2016/06/1.2-Is-Theology-Poetry-Reading.pdf.

I   Benjamin Wormald, "Religious Landscape Study," *Pew Research Center's Religion & Public Life Project*, May 11, 2015, accessed December 10, 2017, www.pewforum.org/religious-landscape-study/belief-in-god/.

J   Bill Webster, "Catholics Say Traditional Families Ideal; Other Family Arrangements Acceptable," *Pew Research Center's Religion & Public Life Project*, August 28, 2015, accessed December 10, 2017, www.pewforum.org/2015/09/02/u-s-catholics-open-to-non-traditional-families/pf_15-09-02_catholicsurvey_families640px/.

K   "What Is Secular Humanism?" *Council for Secular Humanism*, accessed September 25, 2017, www.secularhumanism.org/index.php/3260.

L   Ibid.

M   Charles J. Chaput, *Strangers in a Strange Land: Living the Christian Faith in a Post-Christian World* (New York: Henry Holt, 2017), p. 230.

N Wangqiu, "The secular humanist principle," *Purpose of Life* (blog), December 26, 2008, accessed September 20, 2017, purpose-of-life-1.blogspot.com/2008/12/secular-humanist-principle.html.

O "A Humanist Discussion of… Death and other Big Questions," *British Humanist Association*, accessed January 6, 2018, www.humanismforschools.org.uk/pdfs/death%20and%20other%20big%20questions.pdf.

P *Catechism of the Catholic Church* 1703–4.

Q "The Purpose of Man's Existence," *CatholiCity.com*, accessed September 25, 2017, http://www.catholicity.com/baltimore-catechism/lesson01.html.

R "Definition of Humanism," American Humanist Association, accessed September 24, 2017, americanhumanist.org/what-is-humanism/definition-of-humanism/.

S Based partially upon "Catholic Morality: Life in Christ," *Catholic Morality: A Primer*, accessed January 5, 2018, www.beginningcatholic.com/catholic-morality.

T "What is Secular Humanism?" accessed September 25, 2017, www.secularhumanism.org/index.php/3260.

U "A Humanist Discussion on Abortion," *Humanists UK*, accessed January 8, 2018, humanism.org.uk/humanism/humanism-today/humanists-talking/humanist-discussion-on-abortion/.

V Valerie Tarico, "Why I Am Pro-Abortion, Not Just Pro-Choice," *Council for Secular Humanism*, accessed January 8, 2018, https://www.secularhumanism.org/index.php/articles/8033.

W Arthur Caplan, "When Does Human Life Begin?" Council for Secular Humanism, accessed January

8, 2018, www.secularhumanism.org/index.php/
articles/5639.

X   Robert Kraynak, "Justice Without Foundations,"
      New Atlantis, Summer 2011, accessed September 21,
      2017, www.thenewatlantis.com/publications/justice-
      without-foundations.

Y   Robert Barron, "The Myth of the War Between
      Science and Religion," *Word On Fire*, December 8,
      2008, accessed February 1, 2018, www.wordonfire.
      org/resources/article/the-myth-of-the-war-between-
      science-and-religion/331/.

Z   Ibid.

AA   Theodore Gracyk, "St. Thomas Aquinas: The
      Existence of God can be proved in five ways," 2016,
      accessed February 28, 2018, web.mnstate.edu/gracyk/
      courses/web%20publishing/aquinasFiveWays_
      ArgumentAnalysis.htm.

AB   Thomas Reese, "The hidden exodus: Catholics
      becoming Protestants," *National Catholic Reporter*,
      April 18, 2011, accessed November 21, 2017, www.
      ncronline.org/news/parish/hidden-exodus-catholics-
      becoming-protestants.

AC   Ibid.

AD   Pope Benedict XVI, *God and the World, Believing and
      Living in Our Time: a Conversation with Peter Seewald*
      (San Francisco: Ignatius Press, 2002), pp. 22–23.

RECOMMENDED READING
AND RESOURCES

Listed in order of appearance

Books

Rediscover Catholicism by Matthew Kelly (Beacon
Publishing)
Rediscover Jesus by Matthew Kelly (Beacon Publishing)
The Real Story by Curtis Martin and Edward Sri (Beacon
Publishing)
Catholic and Christian by Alan Schreck (Servant)
Pillar of Fire, Pillar of Truth (Catholic Answers)
Forming Intentional Disciples by Sherry A. Weddell (Our
Sunday Visitor)
The Joy of the Gospel (Pope Francis's encyclical *Evangelii
Guadium*) (United States Conference of Catholic
Bishops)
*Nudging Conversions: A Practical Guide to Bringing Those
You Love Back to the Church* by Carrie Gress (Beacon
Publishing)
Mere Christianity by C. S. Lewis (Harper One)
The Great Divorce by C. S. Lewis (Harper One)
The Screwtape Letters (Harper One)

Something Other than God by Jennifer Fulwiler (Ignatius Press)

The God Who Loves You: Love Divine, All Loves Excelling by Peter Kreeft (Ignatius Press)

Born Fundamentalist, Born Again Catholic by David Currie (Ignatius Press)

By What Authority: An Evangelical Discovers Catholic Tradition by Mark Shea (Ignatius Press)

Crossing the Tiber by Stephen Ray (Ignatius Press)

The Protestant's Dilemma: How the Reformation's Shocking Consequences Point to the Truth of Catholicism by Devin Rose (Catholic Answers)

Rome Sweet Home by Scott Hahn (Ignatius Press)

Surprised by Truth edited by Patrick Madrid (Basilica Press) and *Surprised by Truth 2* and *3* (Sophia Institute Press)

Why Do Catholics Do That? A Guide to the Teachings and Practices of the Catholic Church by Kevin Orlin Johnson PhD (Ballantine Books)

The Lamb's Supper by Scott Hahn (Darton, Longman & Todd Ltd.)

Catechism of the Catholic Church (United States Conference of Catholic Bishops)

Compendium of the Catechism of the Catholic Church (United States Conference of Catholic Bishops)

Humanae Vitae by Pope Paul VI (Ignatius Press)

Theology of the Body for Beginners by Christopher West (Ascension Press)

Good News About Sex & Marriage (Revised Edition): Answers to Your Honest Questions about Catholic Teaching by Christopher West (Servant)

The Universe Next Door by James Sire (IVP Academic)

Finding Truth by Nancy Pearcey (David C. Cook)

Understanding the Times by Jeff Myers and David A. Noebel (David C. Cook)

Catholicism and Reason by Rev. Edward J. Hayes, Rev. Msgr. Paul J. Hayes, and James J. Drummey (plus four other books in the series) (CR Publications)

How to Do Apologetics: Making the Case for Our Faith by Patrick Madrid (Our Sunday Visitor)

Orthodoxy by G. K. Chesterton (GLH Publishing)

Thoughtful Theism: Redeeming Reason in an Irrational Age by Andrew Younan (Emmaus Road Publishing)

Why I Am Catholic (and You Should Be Too) by Brandon Vogt (Ave Maria Press)

Why We're Catholic: Our Reasons for Faith, Hope, and Love by Trent Horn (Catholic Answers)

The Case for Catholicism by Trent Horn (Ignatius Press)

Online or DVD Videos

The Journey Home television show hosted on EWTN by Marcus Grodi. Videos can be viewed for free at chnetwork.org/journey-home/ as well as on YouTube.

Why I'm Catholic website: stories by Protestant converts at: www.whyimcatholic.com/index.php/conversion-stories/content/8-protestant-converts.

Convinced by Don Johnson (Don Johnson Ministries) also available as of 2018 through Formed.org.

Websites and Programs

Amazing Parish (amazingparish.org/)

Be My Witness (a program of RENEW International at
    bemywitness.org)

The Evangelical Catholic (www.evangelicalcatholic.org/)

Rebuilt (www.rebuiltparishassociation.com/)

Catholic Christian Outreach (cco.ca/resources/
    faith-studies-series/)

Alpha (alphausa.org/catholic/)

Light of the World (www.lotwem.org/)

Discovering Christ (christlife.org/)

ABOUT THE AUTHOR

In 1998, Cathy returned to the Catholic Church after spending almost 25 years heavily involved in Protestant churches. Diving wholeheartedly back into the Catholic Church, Cathy worked at her local parish as Director for RCIA and Adult Faith Formation until 2011. She continues to serve as a volunteer in adult faith formation programs, most visibly in the Alpha course and at the "Got Faith Questions" table in the church courtyard.

Cathy is also an author and publisher, primarily focused on reviewing educational resources for the homeschool market at CathyDuffyReviews.com.

Her passion for evangelism springs from her own spiritual journey as well as from encounters with many people who are trying to sort out the important questions about life and eternity.

Everyday
EVANGELISM
for CATHOLICS